Treece, Henry
    Westward to Vinland; illus. by William Stobbs; map by
Richard Treece.   S.G. Phillips, inc. 1967
192p illus map

    This story of the Norsemen tells of Red Eirik who was exiled from
Norway and settled first in Iceland and then in Greenland. "His son, Leif
the Lucky, spurred on by rumors of a rich, empty land, sailed west and
reached America. . . . An attempt to set up a permanent colony failed when
violent quarrels broke out amongst the settlers. A series of misfortunes and
the hostility of the [indigenous] Skraelings finally forced the survivors to
return to Greenland." Publisher's note

1 Eric the Red—Stories   2 Leif Ericsson-Stories
3. America - Disc. & explor. - Stories I. Title
NR 11/68
67W17,921   (W)   The H. W. Wilson Company

WESTWARD
TO VINLAND

Illustrated by William Stobbs

Map by Richard Treece

WESTWARD
TO VINLAND

BY HENRY TREECE

S. G. PHILLIPS, INC. NEW YORK

CONTENTS

PART THREE *The Last Seekers* 113

ILLUSTRATION SOURCES

The following drawings in this book are based on Norse archeological remains: pages 3 and 160, carved animal head, in the British Museum; pages 11 and 142, carved animal head-post from the Oseberg ship, in the Ship Museum, Oslo; page 34, carved wooden utensils from Dalarne, Sweden; page 39, carved animal head in the Danish National Museum, Copenhagen; page 46, bronze brooch in the Danish National Museum, Copenhagen; page 55, silver gilt brooch from Sodermanland, in the Stockholm Museum; page 66, gilt bronze figure from Vestfold, Norway, in the Universitets Oldsaksamling, Oslo; page 71, device for Viking flag, from MS drawing; page 75, animal head from the Oseberg Ship, in the Ship Museum, Oslo; page 83, design on sword scabbard, in the Copenhagen City Museum; page 90, animal carving, in the Universitets Oldsaksamling, Oslo; page 115, bronze mount in the Wisbech Museum, Cambridgeshire; pages 119 and 191, helmet, in the Danish National Museum, Copenhagen, whetstone, in the British Museum; page 131, sword hilt and brooch, in the National Museum of Antiquities of Scotland, Edinburgh; page 151, ivory chessman, in the British Museum; page 156, animal head from the Gokstad Ship, in the Universitets Oldsaksamling, Oslo; page 167, harness decoration from Helsingland, Denmark; page 180, carved animal head post from the Oseberg Ship, in the Ship Museum, Oslo; page 186, carved wooden vessel from Dalarne, Sweden.

THE DATES IN THIS STORY

Many of the incidents in this story are taken from The Greenland Saga *(written about 1190) and* Eirik's Saga *(about 1260). All of the dates are A.D.*

SOME OF THE PLACES IN THIS STORY

SLABLAND: The southeast coast of Baffin Island or a northerly part of the Labrador coast.

MARKLAND ("FOREST LAND"): The country between Slabland and Vinland; the southeast coast of Labrador, or Newfoundland.

KEELNESS: A promontory north of Vinland and south of Markland, perhaps in the Gulf of St. Lawrence.

VINLAND ("WINE LAND"): Perhaps somewhere on the southern coast of New England.

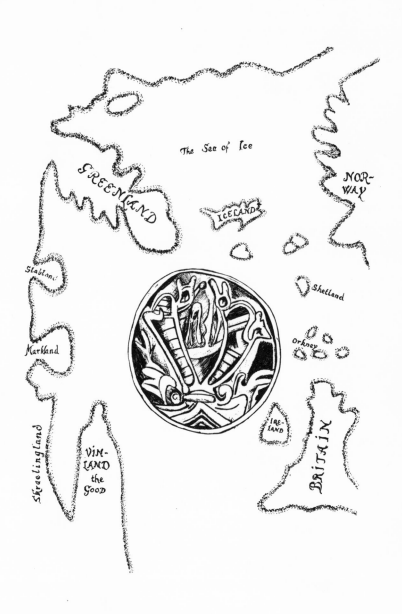

The Sea of Ice

GREENLAND

ICELAND

NOR-WAY

Shetland

Slabland

Markland

Orkney

Skraelingland

VIN-LAND the GOOD

IRE-LAND

BRITAIN

PART I

THE SETTLEMENT

THE MAN-SLAYING

Now Red Eirik was never the man to stay still if an insult came his way. There were many in the hall at Jaederen who were not his friends, yet when the man called Sigurd Sheepshanks taunted him over the alehorn and said, "I have seen many men with red hair before but never one with eyes so close set that he looked like a weasel," then Eirik looked round at his old father, Thorvald, who sat higher up the board, and said, "What do you advise, my father?"

Thorvald Asvaldsson sniffed loudly and rubbed his red eyes, as though this were a matter for some thought. Then, looking over the heads of them all into the smoke that curled up from the hearthfire

and wafted among the rafters, he said in a gentle
voice, "If I were young again and could swing an
ax, and if, when I was so young, such a man as this
Sheepshanks mocked my hair and eyes, then I
would take the ax to him and teach him good
Norwegian manners. I can say no more."

He went back to the alehorn, and so Eirik jumped
onto the table and shouted out, "Sigurd Sheepshanks, I call you out. Come and have your beard
trimmed, little one. It is too shaggy."

Now the lord who was at the top of the board,
called White Rolf, rapped on the oak with his gold-
ringed fingers and tried to smile as he said, "Now,
boys! Now, boys! Good is good enough. More than
that is bad."

But this Sigurd was tearing his hair and yelling
for a sharp sword, and all his mates were fumbling
under the benches for the weapons they had
smuggled in. So Red Eirik strolled off down the
long pine hall and picked up his iron ax from where
it lay beside his father's jacket and cloak. Then he
turned into the room again and called, "I am waiting, Sheepshanks. Find a sword and come out."

Eirik went down under the dripping pines and
swung the ax a time or two to get the feel of it after
the week of feasting. It felt all right. The balance
was good, shaft and head equaling one another. It
gave a light blow, this ax. No good for tree-felling
but risk enough for what the smith had had in

mind. Eirik had faith in this ax and, when Sigurd came running and sweating and swearing, Eirik just nodded to him and took a good post where overhanging boughs would not spoil his swing. Then he said softly, "Do you want the holmgang rules, fighting on a spread hide, or will it suit you here?"

Sigurd yelled, "I cannot wait for a hide, protect yourself, you weasel-haired fox."

Eirik said, "Let us be sensible northmen, Sheep-shanks. You can either call me a weasel or a fox, but not both at the same time. That is not in nature, friend."

Sigurd ran straight at him, whirling his iron sword. His ragged beard was floating in the wind as far back as his red ears, he was so furious. He screamed, "Then I call you fox—and I am the hound that will crunch your red bones."

Eirik said, "We shall see about that," and, when Sigurd swept his long blade outward like a scythe, Eirik bent under it and let the ax blade go from him. The jolt, as the ax struck Sigurd's leg, almost took the ash shaft out of Eirik's hands. Sigurd fell against him almost hard enough to knock him down. The iron sword flew over Eirik's shoulder into the bracken behind. Then Eirik caught Sigurd, who was groaning and trying to stand but could not, and lowered him gently onto the turf.

White Rolf came out then, smoothing his blue

silk feast shirt, and asked, "Have you fellows settled your difference?"

Eirik said, "Aye, lord, it seems that Sigurd has no more to say just now."

"Good," said the lord, turning back, "then let us not waste feasting time. There is still another dish of pork to eat."

Most of the men followed him inside. But four of them kneeled round Sigurd who was sighing deeply, and they showed their white teeth at Eirik as though they were wolves.

Eirik said, "You are his kinsmen, friends, so I expect you to show your white fangs as though you were wolves. But halt a moment and consider that it was Sigurd, not I, who started this."

One of them, wearing a catskin cap, shouted out, "Aye, you did not start it—but we shall end it."

Eirik said pleasantly, "You must suit yourselves. First come, first served. I go to eat the lord's Yuletide pork and cannot stay out here in the cold."

One of them called after him, "You will not be cold for long, axman. We will stoke the fire for you."

And that night, while Eirik lay asleep in his wall bed under the calfskin coverlet, flames roared on his thatched roof and charred beams fell suddenly into his house. He sat up and said to his father, "Hey, our thralls did not put the hall fire out. It has caught in the thatch. I shall thrash them tomorrow and no mistake."

Old Thorvald was standing with his iron sword in his hand. He said, "Never mind about tomorrow —it is now that matters. Keep quiet and bring the ax."

They went outside, keeping close to the cow byre wall. And in the stackyard they saw the four brothers who had kneeled over lamed Sigurd that day. Each man had a pine torch in his hand and all were laughing.

Eirik went one way round them, and his father the other, and what with sword and ax, coming out of the black shadows, they did sharp work very suddenly. It did not need doing twice. When it was all over, they beat the thralls out of their sleep and got them to smother the flames as well as they could, for the house had given itself up to fire by then.

In the morning Thorvald suggested to Red Eirik that they go to White Rolf and explain the matter to him. "A man must protect himself," Thorvald said.

So off they rode to the lord's house. They found him up with his red cloak on, waiting for them. Before they could lodge their charges he said starkly, "You may be right; you may be wrong. But all I can tell you is that there is no room for you in Norway any longer. Choose what you want: my judgment on the spot now—or judgment by the Thing. I will just say that if you choose the latter there will also be blood money to pay to all the kin of those you have injured. And that, I guess, could be about twenty people. I do not know of any man, not even the king, who could pay off twenty people for the loss of their husbands and fathers. So choose."

Eirik nudged his father and said, "You choose, father. I am not well up in the law."

So Thorvald went to the lord and said, "Rolf, give the judgment and let's be away."

The lord smiled and nodded. "That's what it is," he said. "Exile—for three years. You'll have to be away, and quickly, before your enemies get onto the scent. You can borrow a ship of mine if yours needs caulking. But off with you to Scotland or Ireland or Frankland."

Thorvald rubbed his hooked red nose and said, "We'll go in my ship, Rolf. Yours lets water in. You are so busy being the lord you don't go down often enough to the boatsheds. Maybe we will set the prow toward Iceland—and maybe not."

White Rolf said, "Once you get offshore, take your time to decide. Drop the anchor stone and consider a while. But now make haste. And at all events, thank you for your advice about my ship-caulking. I will see that my bailiffs go down to the boatsheds more often in the future. Have a good voyage and, when you come back in three years' time, let me hear what it is like up there in the ice.

I always wanted to go there, but a lord has so much to see to, I never had time."

He sent them off with a gift of two casks of sharp voyage-ale, but Eirik and Thorvald went secretly into his sheep pen and also took eight of his fattest sheep. (They left the skins for him, not being mean men!)

Eirik was not unhappy about leaving Norway. He was young and adventurous, without wife or child to worry about, and a voyage to Iceland where many Vikings had settled sounded good to him. With a fair wind and good weather, four or five days of sailing should bring them there and, tho it was known to be a cold and rugged land, a man could build himself a home and farm the steep hillsides, while the fjords were filled with fish there for the taking.

When the father and son got down to their boat, forty young fellows thronged round it, fighting for the privilege of leaving Norway.

Thorvald shouted out, "You laugh now, but you will groan when the oars skin your hands. We want only hard men, not dreamy boys."

They picked twenty men, and they went to Iceland. It took four days with the lucky tail wind they caught after leaving the skerries. They brought a load of timber with them, so they knew they would be welcome. It was very scarce at that time up there on the bare mountains.

TROUBLE IN ICELAND 2

For a while things could not have gone better. Eirik and his father set up house at Drangar and, what with the hay harvesting and sheep tending, had no time left on their hands. They were happy together, singing as they swung the scythe.

Then, that winter, Eirik went feasting to pass the dark nights through and met the daughter of Jorund Ulfsson, who was also singing in the merry hall. Her name was Thjodhild and he thought she must be the most beautiful woman in Iceland. She was tall and slender, her eyes were as blue as the sea, and her hair was long and straight and corn golden. She wore a blue cloak over a red feast robe with silver lace down the front of it and a belt of silver set with jet and garnets.

Eirik said to her, "If your father agreed, I would marry you and gladly."

She screwed up her blue eyes at him and said, "No one has asked you yet. Besides, I have heard things about you. I should always be worrying when you were away from the house, in case you had got into trouble with your ax. That is no sort of way for a woman to live."

Eirik took her by the hand and said, "If I married you, Thjodhild, I should become a different man. I should put the ax away under the bed in a chest, and all men would call me Eirik the Mild. I swear it."

Just then Jorund Ulfsson came up and said, "I would agree to this marriage, Eirik, provided you moved off southward to Vatnshorn and got yourself a farmstead there. It would prove to me that I had a worker for my son-in-law and not a wandering baresark."

Eirik said, "Nothing would please me better. I will go back to Drangar and arrange everything with my father."

As he went through the door, Thjodhild put her hand on his sleeve and said, smiling, "I am glad you asked, after all. I liked the look of you the moment you came into the feast hall. You are so ugly."

So Eirik went off on his horse merrily, but when he reached the steading at Drangar he could not find his father anywhere. He shouted round the house for a while, then went with a lantern into the sheep byre. There in the straw, with a deep wound in his back, lay old Thorvald.

Eirik carried him into the house and laid him in the wall bed, but there was nothing to be done. Now he knew that Jorund was right, and that he had enemies in Iceland, and that it would be wise to move from Drangar as Jorund had said. They buried Thorvald nearby and Eirik decided to take his stock, his slaves, and the longship and move south where he would be safe.

But first he married Thjodhild. They set up house at Vatnshorn. In a while they had a little red-haired baby and called him Leif. He was just like his father, with the same red ears.

This baby was so sharp-eyed that he caught whatever he reached out for, and once he had it in his hand, whether it was a dangling chain from his mother's neck or a horn spoon that Eirik was waving at him, Leif would not let go. Eirik was pleased about this and said, "There is a true northman in our cradle, wife. He is lucky in his grasping, and hard in his holding. We will call him Leif the Lucky."

But if Leif was lucky his father was not. He was a busy worker and a good farmer, but life would not go smoothly for him, however hard he tried. One day some of his farm slaves were trampling up and down on the hillside, carrying stones for a byre wall, when they started a landslide by accident. Boulders and scree crashed down onto a farmstead belonging to a man called Valthjof. Straightway, this man's kinsman, Eyjolf, ran up the hillside with his sword and killed the slaves, though they cried for mercy.

Eirik was lacing his shoes when he heard the news. One of the thong laces snapped in his hands. He said nothing, but quietly went to the bed and got his ax out. Then, wrapping a blue cloak about his left arm, he went out of the house. When he came back at sunset his wife said starkly, "Well?"

He wiped the ax and put it away, then he went to Leif's cradle to play with him. After a while he said, "Eyjolf will kill no more slaves." Thjodhild bit her lip and asked, "Did you meet him in the presence of witnesses?"

Eirik nodded. "Aye," he said, "he had Hrafn the Baresark with him."

His wife said, "Thor be praised, husband. At least the law-speakers will know that it was a fair fight and not an ambush."

Eirik shrugged his shoulders. "I don't know," he said. "I had to kill Hrafn too; he came at me from behind, with that long sword of his. I never cared for those long swords."

Then Thjodhild began to weep, as well she might. At the next meeting of the Thing assembly, so many Icelanders took up the case against Eirik that he had to leave his new farm and go with his family to Oxen Island. At least, he thought, no one would bother him there.

But he was wrong. He had a farmer-neighbor called Thorgest, who was always borrowing from other men. Now, Eirik had some very beautifully carved and painted wooden panels that he used to set up in the hall over the benches at feast times to decorate the place. It was not long before Thorgest noticed these and his eyes sparkled. "I'd like to borrow those boards," he said. "I am holding a feast this winter and those boards would set off my own benches. They would make my hall look like a king's."

Eirik was anxious to lead a quiet life. "Certainly," he said, "but let me have them back in time for my own Yuletide feast."

Three times he went down to the farm and asked Thorgest for the boards, but each time Thorgest shook his head and said, "I have taken quite a liking to those boards, Eirik. I think I can put them to better use than you can. Yes, I like those pretty boards."

When this was said, Thorgest had all his sons behind him, besides a number of fighting-men who fed from his store. Eirik went home biting his knuckles. He could not sleep for thinking about his feast boards. Thjodhild said, "Husband, you must forget the boards. They are only wood and paint after all, and we cannot afford to get into any more trouble."

Eirik punched at the wall panels and said, "Fair's

fair, wife. They are my boards, wood or not. As for trouble, it is Thorgest who is starting this, not I."

He got up silently in the night, collected some of his men from the byre, and went off to Thorgest's house. At first all went well, but as they were carrying the feast boards away down a little steep valley, Thorgest and his men jumped out on them. Thorgest shouted out, "Now we'll see whose boards they are! I hate a mean lender and you are one."

Eirik called back, "I think you have borrowed from me for the last time, neighbor." Then he set to with his ax. It was a running fight, in the wet darkness, and many hard blows were struck on both sides. But Eirik got his boards back home. As for Thorgest, two of his sons and several of his fighting-men fell in that dark valley and lay with their faces in the water.

When he reached home, Eirik found Thjodhild waiting for him with little Leif in her arms. She was weeping and said, "It was an unlucky day when I met you at my father's feasting. When I married you, I married trouble."

Eirik nodded grimly. "Aye," he said, "that's true enough—but right's right, wife. And you cannot go beyond it. Now pack up a few things while I hold Leif. By dawn Thorgest will come looking for me with all the men he can call out, and I have had enough ax-work for one day."

They went down to the shore in the darkness and

off in the ship to Swine Island, where Eirik knew a friendly farmer. There they stayed in hiding while Thorgest scoured the islands in search of him.

When the next Thing assembly met at Thorsness, all the blame was put on Eirik. As he was a newcomer in Iceland, he had few to stand up for him, so he was declared outlaw for three years.

That night Eirik sat by the fire with his friend and said, "I cannot go back to Norway and I am thrown out of Içeland. If I stay here, any man has the right to kill me. Where can I go?"

His friend said, "About eighty years ago there was an old seafarer called Gunnbjorn who got blown by storms westward from here and found a number of islands. Why don't you go and look for them? The weather there can't be any worse than it is here. Besides, if you stay here someone will kill you. I'd rather live among the ice floes than die beside the warmest fire in Iceland. You have your family to think about as well."

There and then Eirik made up his mind. He stocked his longship with bread, meat, and voyage-ale. He saw that the sail and awning were sound and the ropes strong. He had the planks tarred and took aboard all the furs and sheepskins he could lay his hands on. Word went round secretly, and it was not long before he had a crew of hard-handed young men who wanted to find out what the world away to the west was like.

GREENLAND 3

They sailed off with a good tail wind past the glacier of Snaefells. One of the young men stood by the gunwale and exclaimed, "Ah, there she goes, that old ice rock, and good riddance!"

Eirik glanced back and said, "Before we set foot on land we might remember her white robes with love and wish we could see her again."

At first they saw many ships about them, some fishing, some carrying timber for house-building, and some just lolling on the tide wondering where to go for pickings. But when they were a day out and the green sea rocked round them broad and empty, they saw no ships, though from time to time the waves carried driftwood past them and once

they even saw the carved prow of a longship bob-
bing up and down, its gold all tarnished and its
pretty chisel-work full of green sea-moss.

Eirik gave a shudder and looked back toward Iceland. He could still see the tip of Snaefellsness, very
low on the sea and half-hidden by gray cloud. He
went to Thjodhild where she sat nursing Leif under
the awning and said, "Wife, if we go on we may
all die."

She nodded and smiled. "And if we go back you
will certainly die, Red Hand," she said. "Hold the
prow to the west and do not bother me. I am busy,
as you can see."

Late the next day, while Eirik was at the steerboard, he gazed ahead and then began to rub his
eyes as though they had got mist in them. To one
of the keen-sighted youths he called, "Hey, look
where I am pointing and tell me what you can see."

The youth gazed and said at last, "I think I can
see a very tall mountain, much like old Snaefellsness, only blue."

Eirik nodded. "I am glad you can see it too," he
said. "I thought I was dreaming at first. And it is
blue. That must be the ice on it. We will call it
Blueshirt and head toward it."

The Icelanders all stared then, and pointed, and
began to cheer. But though many white birds came
out to fly round the longship, it was another two
days before they got close enough to see what sort

of land they had come to. There was grass, to be sure, but there was even more gray rock. It was a stark land, with mountains rising out of the cold green sea into a cold gray sky.

Eirik said, "Well, what can't be cured must be endured. At least we know the way back home if we don't like it here."

Thjodhild nodded. "Whether we like it or not, this must be our home for the next three years. Your outlawry will be over then and you can go back as a free man, if you choose to. But I have a feeling that once we can find a sheltered fjord and a ship haven where we can set up house, we may get to like this place well enough."

So, while the weather was still good, they headed southward round the coast. When the winter came they put into a fjord, drew the ship ashore, and then worked at making themselves a house. First they dug a shallow pit in the ground, with steps down to it; then they collected all the loose rock they could and made walls. They anchored the ship's sail over driftwood for a roof, and then covered the whole with turf, to keep out the bitter winds. There they all lived together, feeding on what they had brought, on berries from the bushes, and on fish from the fjord. When the ice came, it closed round them like a cold hand. The ground was harder than iron. They thought that the end of the world had come and that this was the end of the world.

Thjodhild marked off the months with a knife on a stick. At last she said, "Spring should be here soon, and then we can sail on round the coast, husband."

No one believed her, but she was right. And that spring Eirik discovered a green fjord that looked as pleasant as anything he had ever seen, even in Norway. He said, "This shall be called Eiriksfjord, and one day I shall build a farm here and call it Brattahlid. How does that seem to you?"

His wife smiled and said, "I am content. Leif is growing well, and soon we shall have another child to keep him company. You have chosen the name of our farm, I shall choose the name of our child. If it is a boy, he shall be named Thorstein."

And that was how it turned out.

The Icelanders sailed southward round the land and found many inlets and islands, and to each of them Eirik gave a name. Then they went up along the western coast of the land, but here they found too much wilderness and turned back.

Eirik said to one of the men, "It's a hard land, this, but a man could wrench a living out of it if he tried. There seem to be no other men here, and no wild beasts. All we have to fight is the winter."

The man said slyly, "If we ever want other north-folk to come here and help to tame this land, we must keep our mouths shut about the winter. That would frighten them off."

Eirik leaned on the ship's rail and thought a while. He said at last, "When my time of outlawry is over, we will go back to Iceland and collect a few hardheaded families and bring them out here. I will follow your advice, and we will tell them that the land is green and fertile. We will tell them that it is called Greenland. They will think that sounds better than Iceland!"

After this voyage round the fjords, he got back to his own inlet and the stone house to find that Thorstein had been born. He declared him a fine boy and in all ways the right brother for Leif. But Thjodhild said, "Eirik, a terrible thing almost happened while you were away. Leif was crawling about outside in the sunshine, on an oxhide I put out for him, when a big dog came down the hill and began to play with him."

Eirik said, "We brought no dogs with us. I am always glad to hear that there are friendly beasts in a strange land."

His wife looked down at her loom, then said, "This one tried to carry the boy off in its arms, Eirik. One of the men you left behind went out and chopped off its head to save our son."

Eirik said, "Did you keep the head, wife?"

Thjodhild nodded. "It is on the shelf in the outhouse," she said. "It was a big white dog and stood on its hind legs."

Eirik went to look. When he came back he said, "I can only see a bear's head, wife. I cannot see a dog's head."

Then Thjodhild jumped up and said, "This is a frightful land. I cannot stay here with my children. Thor knows what might come down to us over the black hill if we stay here. This is such a place as could breed trolls."

Eirik gazed at her calmly and said, "It is a woman's place to tend the fire, weave the wool, and raise the children. It is the man's to keep his sword sharp and to attend to the trolls. See to your trade and I will see to mine. In the meantime, I am grieved that our silly thrall killed that good white bear. I have never been in favor of bear-slaying. They are good brave beasts and do no harm unless they are provoked. Wolves are a different beast. I should not have said a word if I had found a wolf's head in the outhouse."

Thjodhild began to laugh strangely. "Why, you are a wolf-head yourself," she said. "I should never have married such a man."

Eirik did not behave badly toward her. He only nodded and said, "Each one to his opinion. I have never denied that. Now look after little Thorstein. I shall take Leif out onto the hill and tell him what I have seen voyaging."

He did this, but the boy could not take in much of what his father reported. And when Eirik said,

"And next year, or the one after, I shall go back to Iceland and fetch perhaps twenty shiploads of folk out here," little Leif only laughed in the sunshine. Eirik then put him onto his back and galloped back down the rocky hill to the stone house. Leif laughed all the way home, but was sick when they got indoors.

Thjodhild said sternly, "You are a better hand at dealing with trolls than children, it seems, husband. Get about your business."

So Eirik went down to the fjord and started to fit out the black longship for the trip he would make to Iceland when his time was up.

THE COLONISTS 4

By the time Eirik's outlawry was over, his two sons, Leif and Thorstein, were old enough to keep their footing in the bucking longship. With a west wind in the full sail they made a good crossing and cheered to sight tall Snaefellsness ahead of them. Leif tried to climb the mast; Thorstein ran between the rowers' benches, rattling the hung shields with a walrus tusk.

There was a grim-faced man with shaggy black hair and great shoulders among the crew. His name was Thorhall the Hunter and only Eirik could get on well with him because of his bad temper. All the same, Thorhall loved the boys and said, "If I had two such young hawks for my sons, I would not thank you for the throne of Norway. Mark my words, Eirik, they will grow up to see many things that men have not seen before. Their names will be remembered when ours are forgotten."

Thjodhild, sitting under the prow, said, "You talk like a wild man, Thorhall. As long as they grow to be sound farmers, that is all I want for them. The sea has swallowed too many good northmen already. I want my sons to keep their feet on dry land."

Thorhall laughed and pointed across the green water with his right hand. "Woman," he said, "away to where I point lies Ireland. A man can get good pickings there. Their kings are fools; they hide their gold as squirrels hide their nuts—and forget where it is. And their horses—you have never seen such horses, all fed on the sweet green grass of the place. When the boys are of an age, I will take them there and they shall see what the red gold is like, and what riding a real horse is like."

Thjodhild snorted and said, "I hope they will have more sense than to follow you, when the time comes."

Thorhall the Hunter put up his beard into the sky and laughed. "They'll follow me, woman," he said. "I can make any dog or any brisk young fellow come with me, just by whistling. I can even make the deer come within arrow range by whistling. You shall see, one day I will whistle to these boys, then off we'll go. Perhaps we'll push on beyond Ireland down to Spain where the Caliphs live. They have gold enough, too, and horses. And I'll find them a princess apiece to wed down there."

Eirik said, "That's enough, now, Thorhall. I know the signs. You will get us both into trouble with your jesting. Come aft and take the steerboard and guide us well into Breidafjord haven. See, there are folk waiting to watch us come in. We must make a good showing after all this time."

So Thorhall took the longship in, and the first man they met at the wharfside was Thorgest, with his sword out and fifty stark-faced fellows standing behind him glowering.

He came to meet Eirik and said, "I see you have brought your two sons with you, Red Hand. Do you remember that you once killed two of mine?"

Eirik smiled and said, "I come in peace now, Thorgest. I have paid the price for what I did."

Thorgest said, "Three years' outlawry does not bring back my two sons. I still miss them in my house. But your two sons would ease my pain a little."

Eirik shrugged sadly. "Then you will have to fight for them, Thorgest," he said, dragging out his ax.

He was weary from the voyage and had not yet got his land legs back. He had all he could do to skip and sway to avoid Thorgest's long sword. At last the sharp blade sheared through the ash shaft and Eirik stood weaponless. Thjodhild screamed and hid her face under her black cloak. But Thorhall the Hunter came to the rescue. He sprang up, his black beard bristling, and said, "I will take on the quarrel, Thorgest. Leave Eirik alone now and face me instead."

Thorgest, however, shook his head and said, "I have waited for three years to prove that I am a better fighter than Red Hand here. Now that I have done that, I am content. And my dead sons will be content also. He can keep his life, and his sons, as a gift from me."

Then he and his men turned and strode away through the crowds. Thorhall felt ashamed at it all, but Eirik slapped him on the shoulder and said, "I am not ashamed, so why should you be? I have got a good bargain out of this meeting, after all. Now I can go about the land and collect some brave voyagers without wondering if old Thorgest is going to ambush me in every river valley and from behind every heap of stones. I am a family man, now, Hunter, not the sort of baresark I used to be."

But Thorhall still chewed at his beard in rage. As for Eirik, he went about Iceland telling the folk what a prosperous place Greenland could be if only a few shiploads of cunning farmers would follow him out there and build their steadings. And the upshot was that, by the summer, twenty-five longships set off with him from Breidafjord and Borgafjord, carrying with them supplies, sheep, and cattle.

Only fourteen of the ships sighted tall Blueshirt Glacier; the others went into the sea's jaws or turned back to Iceland. But those who made land elected Eirik as their leader in most things. He set up his farmstead at Brattahlid, toward the top of Eiriksfjord, and most of the families clustered about him, though others went round the Greenland coast and set up their own places, to be independent.

After a while a daughter was born to Eirik and Thjodhild. They named her Freydis, and she was a real Viking's daughter, being comely and brave and afraid of nothing from the time she could walk. Unfortunately as time went on she became very proud and stubborn. If she was offended, she flew into a rage and bore malice afterward. She spoiled her good looks by frowning too much. Her brothers put up with this as best they could, but Leif, who was a carefree boy, never really liked her all his life.

STRANGE LONGSHIP 5

Life was not easy in the settlements, but up beyond
the head of Eiriksfjord men found that the grazing
was good. On Brattahlid, Eirik kept over forty cattle
and many goats, sheep, and pigs that could forage
even on the thin slopes. The summers were short,
but warm while they lasted, and after the settlers
had got into the way of things, they found the best
and most sheltered slopes for their corn-growing
and lifted decent crops from the soil.

One day Eirik got the men together in his long
hall and said, "Well, now you have spent a couple of
winters here and you can see what life is like in
Greenland. So far we have hunted only for our own
larders and have not done badly with meat, milk,

and wool. With thought, we could easily catch more caribou, whales, and seals than we have done, and enough fish to keep us over the hardest winter, if we cure them well."

Thorhall the Hunter answered, "Aye, Eirik, we know that. But we need timber in this woodless land for our houses; we need iron for our axes; malt for our ale—or wine if we could get it!"

Eirik nodded and said, "I was coming to that, friend. If we bend our bows and our backs to it, we could gather furs, fleeces, and hides. We could make thong-ropes. We could trap the fine falcons that abound here. We could pile up the ivory of the walrus and of the whale. These could be almost as good as gold in our bargaining· We have ships enough, and good men to sail them, men who know the way to Iceland and, beyond that, to Norway. It is only a matter of picking the right winds and the calm seas. The distance is nothing. Down here we have no ice to contend with. We are lucky men. Soon we could be rich men too. What do you say?"

There was a man called Herjolf Bardarson who said, "I would be happy enough to set course on these merchant voyages as soon as you like, Eirik. I have not seen my son Bjarni for two years. He was away in Norway trading when we sailed here. Sometimes I dream of him and wonder if he is well. There would be news of him if I went to Iceland."

Eirik said, "Aye, that there would be, Herjolf.

But I cannot spare you from Greenland. Let the younger men go with the furs and ivory. You stay here to lend me your support in the council. They will fetch Bjarni back with them."

So it was left at that. The Greenlanders went off in the spring, their ships weighed down in the water with all the things they could gather. The women and children had woven reed cages for the falcons and had rubbed the sheepskins with pumice till they were as soft as silk.

Before autumn the men were back, laden with all the corn and malt and timber they needed. Ships from Norway itself accompanied them, anxious to build up this good trade. Bjarni, however, was not with them. Herjolf went down to the wharf at Eiriksfjord to see if his son stepped ashore, and came back to Brattahlid with a sad face.

"I fear I shall never see my son again," he said to Eirik. He looked round the farmstead, where Leif and Thorstein were playing with sulky Freydis, and where Thjodhild was suckling their newest son, little Thorvald. And he said, "Eirik, your life has turned out luckily for you with such a brood of children. But I am denied my only son, Bjarni. Every night now, when I sit by the fire with the shutters over the windows, I think that I should sail back to Iceland."

Eirik said, "Leave it a little while, old friend. Sometimes Thor makes us wait for what we want most, and just when we have given up heart he lets us have it. He is testing our endurance. You would not say that you had less endurance than other men, would you?"

Herjolf went away to his wife Thorgerd and sat by his fire at Herjolfsness. He said, "I have come to this conclusion, Thorgerd, that we might just as well forget we ever had a son. We shall see him no more."

Thorgerd took his hand and said, "I do not give up hope so easily, husband. When we sailed out here, did we not bring with us a poet from the Hebrides? And did he not make a prayer that went as follows:

> *'I beseech the pure Master of monks*
> *To guide our journey*
> *And out of the high heavens*
> *To hold his strong hand over me'?"*

Herjolf nodded impatiently. "Aye, the Hebridean did that," he said. "He called his prayer 'The Lay of the Breakers,' I recall. What of it?"

Thorgerd said, "That man is a Christian, did you not know? The lord he prayed to in his song was not our Thor. We landed safely here, did we not, husband?"

For a while Herjolf gazed at her sternly. Then he said, "Very well, put a bar across the door so that no one shall see what we are up to. For the sake of my son Bjarni I will even get on my knees to the Whitechrist."

Now three days later Herjolf and Eirik were strolling along the fjord with the sun on their backs, on their way to look at Herjolf's longship that was drawn up on the shore to be tarred. Leif was walking behind them, listening to all they said but not butting in. They were talking about dull things, such as sheep pastures and fish yields. Leif wondered how men who had fought so much and sailed so far should be contented to talk of sheep and fish. He thought, if Thor lets me grow to be a Viking, I will leave all such things to the women and the thralls. I shall put my dragon prow to the green sea and forget about farming and fishing. I shall go where men have not been before. I shall find gold, and a kingdom, and shall have no fear of meeting monsters in dark forests. And when all that has been done, I shall come home to Brattahlid and tell the folk about it. Poets shall make songs about me, and the king of Norway will get to hear of them in his feast hall and will send for me to sit beside him and drink from his ale cup. All men, even the court baresarks, will bow when I pass and will whisper, "Hey, that's Leif Eiriksson. He's the one who sailed where no man has ever been before."

The men were talking and Leif was dreaming, in

the last sunlight of the Greenland summer, when suddenly the boy saw a brown ship, battered and low in the water, away to the far side of the fjord, its sail full with the sea wind, veering round toward them. He caught hold of Eirik's tunic and said, "Father, hey father, look at the ship. It is not one of ours."

But the men were waving their hands and stood deep in the pool of argument. Eirik brushed Leif's hand away and then went on.

So the boy watched the longship swing round toward them and come bearing down. Many of the shields had gone from the gunwales, and the striped sail was split in two places. It would not hold against a good wind for many more hours. Leif wondered if there were rovers aboard it who had come to rob the settlement and to set fire to the houses. So he tried again and called out, "Father, shouldn't you have a sword in your hand at this moment?"

Eirik turned round and saw the ship. But before he could speak, Herjolf cried, "It is *Wolf-Snout*! I know every plank of her like the palm of my hand."

He began to run into the cold water. Then the longship swayed back from the anchor stone and a red-bearded young man jumped overboard and waded through the fjord to meet him and to clasp him round the neck.

Eirik turned to Leif and said, "Wonders will never cease. That is young Bjarni Herjolfsson, come all the way from Norway. I do declare, I never thought we should see that youth again. Let us go down and greet him. You are old enough to shake the hand of seafarers now, my boy. The sooner you start the better."

STRANGE STORY 6

In the long hall at Brattahlid the folk were gathered. Bjarni sat beside Eirik at the crossboard on the dais, food and ale before him, warm wool on his back, to tell of his voyage.

"Call me a fool, my lords," he said, "but now that I am on dry land, I do not care what you call me. I think I have done what no man has done before me, though whose hand held the steerboard I know not. It certainly was not mine for much of the way."

His father, seated below him, said dryly, "Tell us what happened in plain words, my son. Leave all the magic to the poets who shall tell the tale again at another time. Come, we are waiting."

Bjarni bowed his head and said, "Yes, father. Well, as you know, I was in Norway when I heard that twenty-five ships had set course for this land, so I sailed to Iceland without delay and went up to the old farm on the hillside. I found it empty and my parents gone. Tears ran down my cheeks; I would not stay even to unload my cargo but called the men aboard again and set course directly to the west. I had not sailed the Greenland Sea before, but I knew that if I kept Snaefellsness behind me, I should see Blasark before long. Then it would only be a matter of time, sailing southward round the coast, before I could put in to haven.

"But when we were three days out, and Iceland had sunk behind us, out of sight, the east wind failed and a north wind took its place, blowing us down toward Ireland. Thick fogs came and hung about us for days. We did not know where we lay, so I took down the sail and we bobbed about on the green sea, letting the waves do with us as they wished.

"Sometimes we saw the floating wreckage of other boats, and often at night we heard strange voices calling out to us through the fogs. But we came to no harm. Finally one morning the east wind came again and blew the fog away. Then the sun shone and I could get some sort of bearing. I hoisted the sail and sped before the wind. The next day we sighted land, but it was so greenly wooded and its hills were so low and gentle, we knew it could not be Greenland."

Eirik said, "So, you had circled round in the fogs and had gone back to Norway, Bjarni? But how, with an east wind?"

The young rover flung back his head and laughed. Then he said, "Norway, master! Nay, that belongs to the world we know, the olden world. I have sailed to the other side of the dish and have been to a new world."

Even his father cried out to shame him, like all the others, when he boasted so. But Bjarni held up his hand for silence and said, "Look, all you ship-masters, when I saw this green land, I put off again to sea with the shore to my left hand and, after two days' sailing, came to yet another flat and forested land. Here I had the greatest difficulty because the rowers with me wanted to go ashore for water and firewood. But I told them we had enough of both, and this time I caught a wind from the southwest. Now, even you women will understand this, the wind blew from behind and toward the left, send-ing us toward the north and the right hand. We sailed before this wind for three days, and at the end of that stretch we saw a land full of stark moun-tains and glaciers and slabs of rock. It looked so bare, there was no sense in thinking it would be the Greenland Master Eirik had described to us, so we just went round its coast for a while. And then we found it to be an island."

Eirik put his hand to his brow. "Where you have been, no man will ever know, lad," he said, shaking his head and reaching for his cup.

But Bjarni smiled and said, "I put out into open sea once more, Eirik. My southwest wind now blew a gale. I had the sail pulled down, so as not to risk blowing it to shreds. Now I will tell you what happened: Four days from taking in the sail we saw yet another land, and as the sun came out we sighted a fjord before us. We slackened the sail and went up that fjord and there, on the shore, I saw my father's longship hauled up and men tarring it as though for a voyage. So, I am here."

Herjolf struck the table before him with a mighty clout. "The world is a dish," he said, "just as you guessed, my son. And you have sailed round its lip, coming to Greenland from the south. Why, Bjarni, you are the most famous of men, you have sailed round the world, no less."

Everyone was laughing and shouting at this and the ale was flowing freely. Thjodhild rose from her place by the hearthfire and took Leif's hand. "My son," she said, "you have heard the voyager tell his tale, and I have noticed that you were listening carefully. That is right and proper for a young boy such as you are. But one day, when you are much older, you will learn that these sailing-men dream dreams in the fogs and the winds. At last they cannot tell left hand from right hand."

Leif said gravely, "Bjarni is a most proper sound-brained man, mother. He knows his left from his right. And he *has* been round the world. I believe him."

Thjodhild took hold of one of his ears and pulled it gently. "So?" she said. "The man has been round the world. So?"

Leif scampered away from his mother to his warm wall bed and jumped under the sheepskin covers. "So," he mocked, "when I am old enough to have my own ship, I shall go where Bjarni went too. For, to tell the honest truth, mother, I cannot bear to think that any Viking has been where I have not been."

Thjodhild turned from him sadly and said, almost to herself, "Is it not bad enough to come out to this distant desert of Greenland, where the summer is so short and the winds are so cold?"

But Leif was not listening. He shouted back at her, "And what is more, mother, I shall take old Eirik, my father, with me. He should never be set at this farming all his days. He is a fighting-man and should not be penned in like a worn-out old horse."

Thjodhild did not answer him. But to herself she whispered, "Aye, a fighting-man, and look where that has got us—a stony farm on a bleak fjord forever, with hardly more weeks of summer than there are fingers on a hand."

She just waved to her son at the door, and went to the bower where her loom was set up. There she set to weaving warm cloth for their winter jackets and a new skirt for Freydis, who always wanted to have as much as her brothers did, if not more.

PART II

THE EDGE OF
THE WORLD

THE CHRISTIAN KING 7

In time Leif grew to be a brisk young man who could use the ax almost as shrewdly as his father, and who had learned all that Thorhall the Hunter could teach him. Often he would stand alone above Eiriksfjord and watch the ships coming in from Iceland with corn and timber or sailing out with their loads of furs and fleeces. He grew dissatisfied with trapping the white fox and the loping hare and wished he could feel the boards bucking under his feet and the blown spray harsh on his face. The sound of the sail whipping in the wind was music to his ears. And in the spring, when he looked up into the blue sky and saw the birds coming back as free as air, with no one to stop them, he almost wept.

On one such morning he turned and said to his brothers, "I can take care of myself now. It is time I was on my way."

Thorstein, who had also felt this yearning, looked away from him and did not answer. Thorvald, who was younger, said, "You must tell our mother first."

She was sitting outside the farmstead in the sunshine at her spinning wheel, wearing a gray gown. And when he had finished, she said, "I have been waiting to hear you speak these words for some time, my son. But now that you have spoken them the pain is greater than I thought. I had hoped I might be ready for it."

Leif said stoutly, "A man must do as he must, mother. A man owes it to himself to see the world. Bjarni has seen the world."

Thjodhild nodded. "Aye, and much good has it done him," she said. "His ship lies rotting on the shore. He dare not put out to sea again. His mother tells me he still screams out in the night that the fogs are choking him. He still sees the wrecked ships floating by on the green waves."

Leif said, "I only dream of the gold I should bring back, and the great name of warrior I shall leave behind wherever I go."

Thjodhild drew him to her and put her arms around him. She said, "For your first voyage, I implore you with my hands together, do not go where he went. Do not set the prow to north or to west, my love. There is something waiting for us in this hard land, something lurking in the north and west, dark and frightful, nameless, almost ready to close in on us all."

Leif said, "So far we have met no dangers, mother, apart from the hard winters. You have been dreaming. You spend too much time alone."

Thjodhild said, "If you go, I shall spend even more time alone, my son. I cannot talk to Freydis, she is not a gentle child. She wishes to impose her will on everyone."

Leif laughed and said, "We must get her married off as soon as I get back. When she has a house to run, that will tame her. But I must go."

Thjodhild said sadly, "Something is waiting for us in the north, my son. It will come upon us soon enough—but do not go to meet it. It is a shapeless thing that lives and breathes up among the snows and the ice-bound waters. Its breath sweeps down into my dreams like poor Bjarni's sea fogs. If you must go a-viking, then take the course eastward toward Norway, where decent folk still live."

Leif bowed in obedience, and less than a month later he went with Thorhall the Hunter in a fine new longship with a strong wind at his back. But when they had left old Blasark behind them, Thorhall came to him at the steerboard and said, smiling,

"See all the ships that pass us, going one way or the other? It is like being in the middle of a cattle market. You can even hear what the rowers are saying to one another when the wind swings. A Viking should go alone, out of sight of other men. That is the test of manhood."

Leif said quietly, "Which way shall I steer?"

The troll-faced Hunter smiled and said, "I have an itch to lay my hands on some good red Irish gold from Wicklow. It would make a better cargo to bring back than Norse iron. Pull her round to your right."

Leif did not question Thorhall, and so they altered course and were in empty sea for three days. On the fourth evening they sighted land and ran into a shallow fjord, thinking they had come to Ireland. But they were soon disappointed, for a hundred men came from behind the rocks and surrounded them, hemming them in with sharp iron spears and calling out that they were sea-wolves and should die on the shore straightway.

Just when things looked very bad, a beautiful lady came down the steps, dressed in red and wearing a blue cloak. She had gold rings round her neck and arms and carried a white staff. Her hair was brown with red glints in it like bronze.

When the spearmen saw her, they drew back. She said in a clear voice, "I am Thorgunna, the lady of this island. Who is the captain of this longship?"

Leif said that he was and that they were looking for Ireland and meant no harm. Thorgunna smiled slyly and said, "I have met Vikings before. But you have come to the wrong place for gold, my friend. This is not Ireland. You are in the Hebrides."

Thorhall put on a gentle face and bowed. "Then we will ask leave to put off again, lady," he said. "We will trouble you no more."

But Thorgunna gazed at him with such cold green eyes that even the grim-faced Hunter lowered his head. And she said, "It is easy enough for the fly to get into the spider's web, fellow. It is a different thing for him to get out again."

Thorhall began to bluster, so Thorgunna told her men to take away the oars and sail of the longship. Then she said, "That sort of voice may do very well when you talk to dogs and horses, seafarer, but when you talk to a great lady who is also a witch, then you must mind your manners if you want to keep a tongue in your mouth at all."

Leif stepped forward and said, "Lady, we come from Greenland and do not know the customs down here in the south. Pardon us."

Thorgunna smiled at him and said, "You are a handsome young man and should grow to be a hero, if you stop mixing with rough fellows like this Thorhall of yours. You can come with me to the steading. The others will be put into the byre under guard. I have always wanted to hear news of Greenland."

The spearmen took his sword and shield away, so there was little Leif could do. And the next day the wind changed, blowing away from Norway strongly, so Leif knew that they must make the best of it.

Thorgunna had many brothers and cousins, who took to Leif and sat round him every night when the windows were shuttered to hear of life in Greenland. After a few weeks he became so popular that Thorgunna released the other Vikings and let them wander about the island as freely as they chose. As she said, their weapons were all locked away, they could not leave the island, so why should they sit in the byre uselessly when they might work for their living?

Leif was her favorite, and she showed him how she could turn a pebble into a mouse, and then back again into a pebble, just by saying some words in an old language and waving her white stick. He laughed at this, but all the same was secretly a little afraid of her.

One day, in the depth of winter, he said, "Can you change the winds, Thorgunna, as the Laplanders can?"

She nodded and took a little thong from her pouch. "Which wind would you like?" she asked.

He named various winds, and each time she looped the thong to make different knots in it—and each time the wind changed.

When she had finished, Leif said, "Oh, if only you would give me a wind to Norway and let me sail on freely. How can I grow to be a hero if I am a prisoner here all my days?"

Thorgunna said gently, "I would certainly give you a wind to Norway, if you swore solemnly to return here afterward and marry me, to become the hero-lord of this island."

Now Leif was too young to think of such things, but he was not Eirik's son for nothing. So he smiled and took her hand. "Of course I shall, Thorgunna," he said, "for you are the wisest and most comely woman I have ever set eyes on. And, as a token that I am betrothed to you, I shall give you a gold ring, a walrus-ivory belt, and a green cloak of wool woven on my own mother's loom up in the north. These will be binding gifts."

Thorgunna gazed into his eyes a long while, but Leif kept his own stare steady and his lips smiling. So in the end she said, "So be it. I believe you. The day after tomorrow I shall raise a wind for you, and you will set sail for Norway. But woe betide you if you break your promise to me, for then a great misfortune will come on your family, and I shall send someone after you, even as far as Greenland."

Leif laughed at this and kissed her cheek. It was as cold as the ice at Brattahlid in winter, but he was a brisk fellow and made no sign that he was afraid of her. And, as she had promised, Thorgunna raised a westerly wind, so that soon the Vikings were on their way toward Bergenhaven.

Thorhall said to Leif, "I could not have done better myself, lad. Well are you called Leif the Lucky. Let's see if your luck holds in Bergen, for they tell me that the King there is a Christman. His name is King Olaf Trygvasson, and he is a very stark man to deal with by all accounts." They made a good landfall and stepped ashore in Bergen to be greeted by King Olaf's men.

When Leif stood before the king in his long dark hall, he thought at first that here he had met his match, for Olaf was a big dark-browed man who glared more like a troll king than a Christian monarch. He always carried his sword and shield and, though he spoke gently to everyone, Leif knew that this King Olaf was not a man to offend. Thus, when in the feasting that evening Olaf said, "You are too brisk a fellow to go on worshipping old Thor, you should be properly converted and christened," Leif smiled and agreed. Olaf sent for his bishop straightway, and when Leif and his comrades left that feast hall, they were all Christians. All except Thorhall, that is. He broke into such a sweat when the holy water was sprinkled on him that his head steamed. King Olaf saw this and said dryly, "Well, here is one that has escaped the net. But he looks too good a man to knock on the head, heathen or not. You must try to convert him on the voyage home, Leif Eiriksson. Will you do that?"

Leif said he would, but all the time he spoke he kept his fingers crossed so that Thor would not hold it against him.

Then the king said, "I need a good missionary to spread Christ's word through Greenland. You shall be that man, Leif. I shall rely on you, do not forget. See that you do not fail me, for my arm is a long one. This is one oath you cannot break. Do not forget."

After that King Olaf gave Leif many presents, but the most valuable of them all were two Scottish slaves, a man and wife called Haki and Hekja. They were swifter than the deer at running and were the best spies and message-carriers in the north. And before Leif sailed back to Greenland, he picked up another friend—an elderly German from Bremen called Tyrkir, who was a clever craftsman at carving either wood or ivory. Such a man would be of the greatest value in Greenland, decorating ships' prows or carving the walrus tusks that the traders took to Iceland for the summer fairs there.

So, when the year turned and the sailing weather got better, Olaf wished Leif Godspeed, and he set course homeward. During that voyage a strange thing happened: As they were rounding the Greenland coast, a great wind came out of the north and swept them out of land sight for some days. Thorhall said that this was because they had become Christians, and some of the men in the longship straightway asked Thor to forgive them and threw their little wooden crucifixes overboard to the sea.

Leif was angry at this, but he knew better than to offend Thorhall. Moreover another event made him forget his anger. Out in the middle of the sea, in the fog, men could be heard shouting in terror. Leif ordered his crew to steer toward these shouts and soon four men could be seen clinging to a rocky skerry while the waves tried to wrench them away. These men were half-dead, and their clothes had all been ripped off by the hungry sea. Leif took the men aboard, and when they had eaten and drunk and had put on warm sheepskins, their leader told him that they had been to the edge of the world and had seen a land where wild wheat grew in abundance, together with vines and maple trees. But when they had tried to get back to Iceland, the winds had taken them and flung them onto the skerry, where their ship had gone down without a trace.

After he had heard this, Leif went to the after-cabin and sat gnawing his knuckles. Thorhall came to him and said, "There is no mistake about it, lad, there *is* something out there to the far west. First Bjarni, now these poor fools tell us. I shall not rest till I have been to see for myself."

Leif nodded. "Aye, Hunter," he answered, "that

is in my mind too. But first I must fulfill my oath to King Olaf. I do not mind breaking my word to a witch, however pretty she is, but a king is something different. And I did not like the look of that long iron sword he always carried over his shoulder. That sword could reach as far as Greenland, and farther."

Swarthy-faced Thorhall laughed then. He said, "I'd back old Thor's hammer against Olaf's sword any day. But each man to his own sort of fish. As for me, I'll stick to old Redbeard Thor. He has never let me down yet."

After that they had good luck and got safely into Eiriksfjord even before their ale had run out.

THE CHURCH
AT BRATTAHLID

8

Leif's mother was so glad to see her son back safely that she accepted Christ as soon as Leif told her of his promise to the king. She said, "At last I have something to believe in that might send away the bad dreams I have. The Whitechrist will fight the terror that grins at me from the northern wilderness every night."

She set the folk to gathering rocks and building, and only two hundred paces from the steading at Brattahlid she had a little church set up. It was not a grand church, and was only sixteen feet long, but its walls were four feet thick and it would stand forever, she said. Close to it she had a graveyard walled around, with enough space in it to bury a hundred folk decently. And when she had done this, Thjodhild made a habit of praying regularly and of shutting herself away from other folk, so that she could prove to the Whitechrist that she meant every word she said.

Red Eirik did not take well to this. He said to Thorhall, "Is she my wife or is she not? When she prayed to Thor she did as I said. Now she has a mind of her own."

Thorhall shrugged his shoulders and said, "No good can come of these newfangled ideas, Eirik. This Whitechrist is sweeping the northlands as far as I can judge, and before long you and I will be spoken of like wild beasts. I can see the time coming when, if a man goes out with a sword across his shoulder, he will get clapped into jail. Men will get to be too soft, with all this gentle praying."

Eirik slapped him on the back and said, "Well, old friend, as long as we can keep going in the old ways, we will. I'm not having any young dog coming back to Greenland with these women's ways to ruin my hardheaded settlers. And when my daughter Freydis marries the man she has chosen, little Thorvard of Gardar, I'll see that she makes her wedding vows before Thor's image, and not before the gentle man on the cross."

But Eirik did not have his way. Freydis was married in her mother's church, with Leif acting as the priest, although it must be said that while the ceremony was going on Freydis kept her right fist clenched, so as to let Thor know that she still believed in his hammer, as her father did. As for Thorvard of Gardar, he had a silly pale face and teeth like a rabbit's, and he was too afraid of women to disobey Thjodhild in her black habit. So he took all the Christian vows and did not dare to clench his fist. In fact, never in his life did that slight man clench his fist other than to hold his porridge spoon.

When all of this was over, Leif went to Eirik and said, "Look now, old one, times change. Let's have no more sulking. You used to be the Red Hand in this family but, now that I have seen a bit of the world, I am quite prepared to look after this house while you go into the chimney corner and tell yourself tales of what you used to be."

Eirik would have taken this from no one else in the world. But he looked at his son's thick red beard and he burst out laughing. "Thor, Thor," he said. "You may call yourself a Christman, son, but you were not given that beard for nothing. Very well, call your god what you like; we are still friends. Now what is on your mind?"

Leif said, "Only this: I am going to the west to see what these rovers are talking about. Twice I have heard about this green land they have seen out there, and if I don't go and look for myself, I shall end up as shriveled and weaselly as this Thorvard, my new brother-in-law."

Eirik said, with one eye on Thorhall, "A bird in the hand is worth two in the bush, Leif. You could end out on a lonely reef, with the green water biting at you and the fogs smothering your cries for help."

But Thorhall was looking away over the fjord, so Eirik got no support from his old bailiff. Then Leif said, "Did you stop to consider what might happen to you when you went to fetch your bench boards back?"

Eirik nibbled his graying beard and then shook his head. "I was young and brisk with the ax then, lad," he said.

Leif said, "And now you are a little older and, because you are more cunning with age, you do not need to be so brisk and jump about so much. You wait and let the other man come to you. Or am I mistaken? Have I got a tired old bull for a father?"

Thorhall began to roar with laughter. Eirik looked stark and said, "Thor's bones! Thor's bones! If you weren't my oldest son, I'd see what was inside your skull for that."

He was jumping about on the hard turf like a madman.

Leif turned to Thorhall and said, "He could still knock a horse down, this old man." Now he was laughing again.

Thorhall nodded. "Aye," he said, "I never doubted it. The three of us are the only northmen left. Not counting your sister Freydis! Now, she has a touch of the old Red Hand in her, as that little husband of hers will find out."

But Leif pushed him aside. "I do not care for that girl," he said frowning. "She will bring trouble to somebody before she is finished. I'm going down to see Bjarni and to buy that ship of his. If it made the voyage to the edge of the world once, then it can make it twice. A good ship knows the way."

Eirik stared after his son, shaking his head. "What can you do with a young stallion like that?" he asked. "By God, to see him and hear him is like living my own life all over again."

Thorhall gripped him by the shoulder and said, "That's the way, old comrade. We will go with him and keep him on the right course, and we will have our youth again. That is what sons are for, didn't you know?"

Eirik smiled sadly. He said, "Now I know why my old father Thorvald went round with me so much, to feasting and fighting. I am sorry he died alone in that barn at night. I should have been there with him, fending off the ambushers. Thank you, Thorhall, for teaching me good northern sense. I will sail to the end of the earth with my dear son Leif, though he calls himself a Christian."

THEY START OFF 9

The upshot was that Leif bought Bjarni's longship from him, had it repaired and, after asking Bjarni many questions about winds and currents, set to and found himself a crew of thirty-five seasoned rovers to sail in it. In this he had no difficulty, for many of the young men were only too anxious to be away from Greenland, to have the joy of sailing, and to see the place where wheat and vines grew without any hard work at tending them.

Leif's brother Thorstein was the worst of the lot. He thought of nothing else but the journey they were to make to the world's edge. But Thjodhild, on her knees praying most of the day in her little stone church, cast cold water on their voyage. She said, "Better to go to Iceland and build churches there, Leif my own. Nothing but bad can come out of all that fog and those treacherous skerries. Mark my words, you will end up on one of those rocky places, howling your head off for Christ to hear you, with only the green water about you, and the fogs over you, and the wicked birds laughing at you. But I tell you this, you shall not take my youngest son with you into perdition. Thorvald shall stay with me at Brattahlid. And, little as I like her, so shall Freydis. I cannot lose you all at one swoop."

Leif hugged his mother and said, smiling, "You are welcome to both of them, Thjodhild. But mark my words too. One of these days I can picture you asking when we shall set forth again, so that you can see the edge of the world with your own eyes. Who knows, you might build churches galore up and down those sunny coasts, with the vines growing over their roofs and the golden wheat pushing into the nave!"

Thjodhild gave him a stern look and went back to her prayers. "Never," she said. "This is my place. Here I am, and here I stay. The Whitechrist would not wish me to move away from Greenland now, I know. What he wishes for your father, I do not know. I can only hope that Red Eirik will come to his senses and be baptized, and will forget this mad idea of voyaging again."

Half of her prayer was answered in a strange

way, though Eirik never became a Christian. As the voyagers set off down to where the longship gnawed at its moorings by the fjord, Eirik's horse suddenly reared at a fox that started from the tall grasses and flung him onto the ground. Leif rode back to him and said, "What, are you so tired already that you will not get up? Do you want us to carry you, old man?"

But Red Eirik groaned and held his side. "I think one of my ribs has been broken on this hard ground," he said. "And my shoulder seems to be out of joint."

Leif got off his horse and stood over him. The sweat stood out on Eirik's face and head. Eirik said again, "This is as far as we shall go together, son. Now I know that I was never meant to discover any land other than Greenland. Old Redbeard has spoken to me in his own rough way."

Leif nodded gravely. "There is more in old Thor than I believed, father," he said. "Certainly he leaves one in no doubt when he speaks, in the way he speaks."

As the thralls carried Eirik back to Brattahlid on a cowhide, he called after Leif, "I shall be with you in spirit, son. I shall eat out my heart until you come back up the fjord. Take old Thorhall as your adviser in all things to do with voyaging. And accept the German, Tyrkir, as your foster father in place of me. He is no fool; he will give you good advice. I have had some long talks with that man about what is what."

Leif bowed before his father's words and went aboard the longship he had bought from Bjarni. Then, with the wind at their back, they went off down the long fjord, singing merrily all the way to the open sea. Even the rowers sang, as though the slip and slide and drag of the ashen oars were a pleasure to their hands and not a penance.

Thorhall whispered slyly to Leif the Master, "Nay, lad, but these Vikings could teach any Christian choir of monks a good lesson in singing! I am all for the gay rowing songs, not those dreary old dirges droned down the nose after long fasting."

Leif said smiling, "I'll not deny you could be right. On the other hand, I'll not agree. I can still remember old Olaf's long iron sword, mate! But let us stop this talk of religion, it spoils the good voyaging."

And German Tyrkir came up and said in his thick voice, "When you are as old as I am, Leif, you will know that it does not matter too much. All that matters is for a man to be a man and not a brute."

VINLAND THE GOOD 10

Tyrkir of Bremen sat whittling a stick under the mast. He said, "It is all very well to sing going down the green-banked fjord. It is another thing to make carols when the sea puts its green fangs round the throat. The songs are pitched on a higher note then. One could mistake them for screams."

One of the oarsmen, a youth from Orkney called Kol, said sneering, "Stick to your sticks, we'll row to our songs, German. There was never an old man but he warned of grief."

Tyrkir nodded to him and said, "I have reared wolf cubs that could have taken your head in their jaws like a plum and not have noticed they had eaten."

Kol lost his stroke on the oar and got cursed by the men on either side of him. He said, "I shall not forget that, Tyrkir, when it comes to landfall-reckoning."

Tyrkir said, "Suit yourself, my boy. I shall not be running away."

Thorhall, beside Leif at the steerboard, said smiling wryly, "I have taken a great fancy to your foster father. He may not be much with the sword and ax, but he is a proper man. We shall advise you well between us, the German and I."

Leif said, "I have no doubt about that, fat-nose. You are very fond of giving advice."

Then the wind swung as they came into open sea and took the steerboard round against Leif's pulling, leading them eastward. Thorhall and Thorstein lent their weight on the elm handle, but they could not beat the sea drag. Leif said, "Enough is as good as a feast. If we do more we shall have our shoulders wrenched out. Let her go and we'll come back to it later."

They drifted and wallowed and soon the fogs closed in on them. The next day when the fog lifted they saw they were back in sight of old Snaefells-ness. Thorhall said, "I'm not going ashore there to be made a song about. Give me the elm-haft, boy, and I'll swing her about or break my arm."

Leif gave him the helm, and Thorhall wrestled with it for a time. At last he grinned and said, "Now we are set right. It needs a seaman to steer old *Wolf-Snout*. This is not one of your narrow-hipped barges —it is a true Viking's ship. It will only obey a big man, one who could wrestle with bears."

But when they sighted flat green fields and sea gulls following the ploughmen inland, even Thorhall said, "Well, this is like nothing but Ireland, lads. I must have given the stick a turn too far. Shall we go ashore and ask them who the king is?"

Leif said sternly, "I am this ship's master, baresark. And while it is afloat I am the king here. Now that you know where we are, set our nose toward western Greenland and I will take over from there."

And this Thorhall did, though with bad grace since he still had his mind set on Wicklow gold. But inside three days Leif said to him, "Right now, I think I can smell the Greenland shoals and tell the color of the water up here. Go aft and sleep. I will take the steerboard."

Two days later he called out to all and said, "Look, away to steerboard, all those slabs of rocks lying about on the headland. This is somewhere else than Greenland. This is Slabland, the place Bjarni saw."

Tyrkir said, nodding over his knife, "Aye, it is Slabland. But I have no wish to land there."

Thorhall, who was sleeping, woke and said, "I just saw a fox scampering across the gray rocks. I shall come here another time to get my furs."

Then the wind came from the north and almost lifted them out of the water. It roared round them like heat from a furnace and Leif said, "Ship your oars, boys, or we shall have nothing left but firewood."

For two days the wind kept at them. On the third the watch-out man called, "Hey, hey, dead ahead, look at the green woods! Look at the white-sand beaches!"

Leif looked and said, "This is good—but not good enough. This we will call Markland. I see the woods and the shores, but I do not see the vines. We shall go on."

Then Thorhall came aft and stood over him, saying, "Are you daft, lad? This is no land I ever saw. This must be the edge of the world. If we go further we shall fall over the lip of the dish into the everlasting darkness."

But Leif was feeling lucky now and said, "Right, we shall fall. Would the falling darkness be any worse than Greenland through the winter?"

Thorhall said, "If anyone but you had said that, I would have put my ax onto his head."

Leif said, "That is no way to end an argument, friend. Then you would not know what the truth was. Only I would know."

Old Tyrkir, under the mast whittling, said quietly, "He would know as much truth as you did, son. I should put my ivory knife under his ribs, ax or no ax."

Thorhall heard him and smiled. "You take things too seriously, German," he said.

Tyrkir answered, "Aye, and I need to, with men like you about."

But there was no real quarreling, and in two days the voyagers saw something they never forgot, however long they lived. There was land before them, with an island standing off it, all lush and green in the sunlight, with the deep blue sky over all. The men stopped rowing, shipped their oars, and gazed astounded. Those of them who had been born on Greenland had never seen such a paradise, for this place swarmed with white geese, green trees, low hills, shoals of fish, and fluttering moths. Even Kol of Orkney said, "Well, Leif, I see no vines or wheat —but any man who went past this place into the utter darkness would be a madman, and I would not go with him. Put into haven here, or I shall jump overboard and take myself ashore."

Most of the others said the same. So Leif headed round the island and toward the mainland. When he had gone a way, he saw that they were at the mouth of an inlet or river, so he went on along it against the deep blue stream, and at last they came to a great peaceful lake, surrounded with tall dark-green trees. Around them the waters swarmed with fish, and birds flew everywhere.

The Vikings jumped waist deep into the water and dragged the longship ashore, laughing and singing whatever came into their heads.

Leif said, "Well, whether it was the Whitechrist or Thor who brought us here, I do not care. If this is the edge of the world, then those who live on its center are getting the worst of the bargain."

Among the tall grasses, they saw red and blue flowers of such delicate coloring that they almost wept. Deep scarlet butterflies fluttered among the flowers, and wild bees, heavy with honey, droned from stem to stem. A family of plump brownish birds, like partridges, stopped and stared at the Vikings without trying to escape. A lazy young brown bear, with his muzzle all sticky from honey, came out from a hole in a green bank and made a playful dab at Thorhall with his paw. Thorhall stepped aside quickly and said, "Hey, comrade, take care. You will rip my best leggings off me, boy. Will your father make me another pair?"

The rovers laughed at the bear's bewildered expression. Then they passed on to a flat place by the shore where Leif pointed and said, "This is where the houses shall be built."

They made the huts of stone and turf, cut with their swords and axes from the mild soil, and roofed them with tarpaulins from the ship. When the houses were complete, they made rods and lines and stood in the lake and caught the biggest salmon on which they had ever set eyes.

As they sat about their many fires in that settlement, Leif said, "King Olaf spoke much about

Heaven. But if it is better than this, I shall be surprised."

Thorhall scratched at his beard and said, "Well, I have never taken the end of life too seriously, boy, but I do not think that I would change this for the Valhalla our bards sing of. Let us stay here."

And all the Vikings shouted, "Aye, let us stay here."

Only old Tyrkir the German was dissatisfied. He said, "Friends, we came here to discover the new lands that Bjarni saw on the rim of the world and to taste the good wine of Vinland. But I see no vines, and I shall not rest easy in my mind until I have."

Leif said, recklessly, "Well, if you would like to go and look for them, foster father, you are at liberty to do so. Never say that I forbade you."

So Tyrkir filled his skin flask with fresh lake water and went off toward the west. The others carried on with their feasting and forgot about him for the time being.

But the next morning Leif was in a fury. "Where is Tyrkir?" he yelled. "Has no one had the sense to go out and look for him? Don't you fools understand that he is an old man and could easily fall into a hole or have a fit or something? Well, this decides it, you are not capable of being left to decide for yourselves. Now you will obey me in all things. Divide into two parties, and one of you go west and the other east. If, by the day's end, you have not found my foster father, then God help you, for I shall have every second man flogged."

Even Thorhall looked shaken at these words. He helped to select the men for the two parties and then gave them the order to set off. But just as he spoke, they saw old Tyrkir come staggering out from a dense wood at the far side of the lake. He walked like a sick or wounded man.

Leif said grimly, "Someone will suffer for this, and no mistake." Then he went into his hut and buried his head in his blanket.

And at last Thorhall brought Tyrkir in to Leif and said, "The wound he has will heal itself, ship-master. I have suffered the same sickness many times, after the Yuletide feasting. See, he cannot walk without help, but he has shed no blood at all." Thorhall was laughing.

Then Leif looked up into Tyrkir's watering eyes. The German said thickly, "Hey, old Leif, I found the vines. Yes, the vines I found. And what rich vines! What wine they made in the sun, unpicked."

He fell onto the bed, looked up at Thorhall, and said, "Truly we have arrived at the destination we sought. This is indeed Vinland the Good. Aye, this is Wine land. Here life will be one long feast."

THORHALL'S WARNING 11

They built more houses by the lake, roofed them with timber from the woods, and spent the winter in Vinland. The climate was so mild there that the grass scarcely withered as the year turned and there were no frosts at all. Men walked out at Yule-tide without their hide jerkins. Some of them even wore no shirts as they fished, thigh deep in the lake's blue waters.

Thorstein came to his brother Leif and said, "I have never known Norway or even Iceland, so I cannot judge what a land should be like. But I can tell you, brother, that this is so fair a place, I would happily stay here for the rest of my life."

Leif clapped him on the shoulder and said, "Aye,

brother, and I hope that we may. But first we must go back to Greenland and tell the folk there what we have found. Our father isn't getting any younger, and I'd like to see our Red Hand sitting in the sunshine for a few years before he goes to wherever such an old heathen goes."

Thorstein laughed in the blue sunlight and said, "Aye, and our mother should build herself a good church here, with the timber that lies so easy to the hand. In this gay place she will forget her dreams of ice and terror coming down from the north. Shall we go back and fetch them, as soon as the winds start blowing up from the south?"

Leif nodded, then went away and set the men building a tow boat of fir wood, so that he could take a heavy load of timber home. He also got Tyrkir to transplant in tubs some of the vines he had found, so that the Greenlanders could taste these wonderful fruits.

Only Thorhall the Hunter had any doubts about it all. He was in a bad mood that day. He screwed up his dark face and said, "Lads, in this life no man ever gets without giving. You will find that this Vinland is not the soft place of dreams you think. You will find that it will ask its price before we have done."

Thorstein said, "Why, you croaking old raven, you!"

But Thorhall answered, "You were only a baby

when I fetched you out of a bear's mouth near the western settlement, Thorstein. In truth, you do not even remember that I did so. I can tell by your eyes. But I did, and asked no reward for it. I may be getting old; I may be a hardhanded ax-swinger and not a Whitechrist wafer-gobbler—but I have seen some life and death in my time. I have seen great kings come and go. They come with their cloaks flying like the clouds at sunset; they go like a little drizzle of gray rain, hardly noticed."

Leif nodded and frowned with impatience. "Come, come, baresark," he said, "we know all this. You have said it all our lives. What do you want to tell us that is new?"

The Hunter said shortly, "You have asked for it. I shall give it to you, Leif, since you are the master of this trip."

"Aye, do that," said Leif, smiling into the sun and pushing his fox-fur cap onto the back of his red head.

Thorhall said, chewing a grass stalk, "This place will kill many of us—whether we go back or stay here. We have found it, whereas it had been a secret place. Soon we must pay the price for finding it— whether we go or stay. Thor did not put it here to be pried into. I shall say no more. But when death comes, remember my words."

Thorstein laughed at him and said, "You are not the only old counselor with us, you know. There is

Tyrkir the German. He knows a few things too. He has not sat by the fireside all his life."

Thorhall nodded unsmiling and said, "Then go to him and ask his opinion." Then he walked into the lake and without even trying caught three salmon in his bare hands.

Old Tyrkir was carving the prow of the tow boat with a chisel he had made of copper. He wiped his brow and said, "Aye, the old baresark is right enough. This place will kill you."

Then he laughed at the young men's faces and said, "And so will any place, lads. For it is man's nature to die in due course, whatever heaven he finds for himself. We cannot drink the good wine forever, now can we? Every feast must end!"

They began to laugh then, and he went on chiseling. And soon after spring broke, they set off for Greenland, having covered Leif's houses well against storms. The journey was so tireless they wondered why half the world was not there in Vinland, drinking the good wine, eating the good bread, catching the fat fish.

They never lost sight of land for a week, with the good breeze at their back and the warm sun over them. When they had come alongside Slabland again, Leif said, "Well, now we should swing to steerboard and cross into the open sea." Then, just as though some god had heard him, the wind changed and took them where he wished.

And when they had been going strong into the green waste for two days, with almost a gale behind them, they saw a jagged reef on the horizon. As they approached it, they made out a longship lying smashed on the rocks and about fifteen folk standing among the jagged black teeth, waving like madmen to them in case they swept on.

Leif said, "It is a good thing we came this way. These folk would have been clawed off their steading by the green fingers before long."

He lowered the sail and the men back-paddled to keep *Wolf-Snout* on the rein; then he put off in the small boat and fetched the stranded folk in, making three trips back and forth.

They turned out to be from Norway. Their captain was a brown-haired youth called Thorir, who had with him a most pretty wife called Gudrid. Her hair was the color of sun-bleached hay and her eyes were the dark blue of cornflowers. Thorstein said to Leif, "It is wrong to envy a man of his holdings, brother—but I tell you, I wish I had been first on the scene when this beautiful lady chose a husband."

Leif thumped him on the chest and said, "Why, you must be even sillier than I thought. A wife like that is not for men like us. We do not need pretty dolls in our houses; we need big-armed corn-scythers and bread-makers."

The brothers almost came to quarreling about this, but just then Thorhall came up to the after-awning and said, "These folk we have picked up, they are not well." Tyrkir who stood behind him said, "I do not like their pale skins, mottled with red. The eyes of some of them seem sunk into their heads and are all black rimmed."

Leif said, "So would your eyes be sunk into your head, old Bremen, if you had been through what these poor souls have. Night after night on a small reef, with all the world's green sea roaring about you. Nay, I shall take them into haven up Eiriksfjord, and that is the Christian thing to do."

Black-browed Thorhall said, "Aye, it may be your soft Christian thing to do, but it is not what I would do."

Thorstein said, "Well, then, old heathen, and what would you do, in your great wisdom?"

Thorhall said, "I should pitch them all back into the sea without any delay, master. And when I had done that I should see that my shipboards were scrubbed clean with fresh salt water. I should scrub them till I had half worn them away, oak or not."

After that he and Tyrkir stuck together, not going near the Norwegians at all. Gudrid was merry enough, but the others lay about by the prow and were not very interested, even when *Wolf-Snout* nosed up Eiriksfjord.

There was much feasting when the news got round that Leif had come home again, and with a tow boat so laden with timber, vines, and furs.

Thjodhild wept without stopping, to see her sons again. Even sullen Freydis kissed her brothers as though she bore them no grudge for being men.

But Eirik came from the feast hall late that night and meeting Leif by the stackyard wall said, "Why did you not throw them back into the sea, as you would if you caught a rotten fish?"

Leif said, "You have been talking to that heathen Thorhall, father."

Eirik said, "I do not need to talk to Thorhall on such matters. I do not need him to tell me what the plague looks like."

Leif said, "These good folk from Norway? These shipwrecked folk? I do not understand."

Eirik said, "Then I will tell you, my son. They were trying to escape a plague that has swept Bergen. But though they went to the edge of the world, it caught them up at the end. You should have left them on their reef, where good Thor had put them for safety's sake. Now, by your Christian meddling, you have brought their disease into our clean settlement."

He turned and went away. Leif did not follow him.

THE PLAGUE 12

The next day the rescued Norwegians began to fall to the ground, wherever they were—sitting at table, walking by the fjord, or helping to pen the sheep. A thrall came running to Thorstein and said, "Master, the Norse captain Thorir has died with his head in his wife's lap and she is crying out for you. Will you go to her?"

Thorstein said, "How can I refuse? I helped to bring them here. I cannot turn my back on them now."

Leif heard this and said to the thrall, "Gather all the men who will go with you and drag the dead Norwegians to the icehouse, away from the steading. Prop them against the outside wall until we have time to bury them decently. I will go to my mother and father and tell them to keep well away from it all."

When he told them, Thjodhild straightway put on her black gown and cloak and said, "I shall go to my church to pray for us all. Do not try to disturb me at my prayers for anything. I shall not come out."

Freydis hurriedly packed a bag of food and warm clothing. "I shall not stay to suffer a death I did not ask for," she said. "I shall go onto the clear fjord water in a skiff with my husband Thorvard of Gardar. If you were wise, Eirik, you would come with us and save your life."

Red Eirik glowered at her and said, "I have never run away from danger in my life, and I shall not start now. Go where you like, Freydis, but I shall stay in my place, here, where I belong."

Thorvard of Gardar showed his teeth and said, "Then you will not stay long, father-in-law. You would do better to follow the wise counsel of Freydis. She is a woman of great wisdom. I always follow her advice."

Red Eirik stared at him bleakly and said, "Do not lecture me, rat-face. Go and catch yourself a little mouse for dinner."

Leif said, "He will never forgive you for that, father. Those hasty words could bring sorrow to someone."

Eirik shrugged his shoulders. "He can suit himself," he said. "I have the feeling in me that I shall not long need his forgiveness, or anyone's."

Then he began to cough and sneeze and sway in his chair. Leif went to him, but Eirik tried to push him away and said, "It is a strange thing, but I always thought that when it came it would come with an ax edge or a sword point or a blow upon the head with a club. When my horse reared and saved me from the sea by giving me broken bones, I did not realize that old Redbeard meant me to stay here and wait for plague to take me. Aye, lad, it is strange. Very strange. Don't let them put me in the churchyard, though. Let my old friend Thorhall have the dealings with me. He knows how."

Then Red Eirik gave a deep groan and fell backward into the straw, without a wound upon him save the red blotches of the plague.

Stunned for a moment by their father's death, Leif and Thorvald stood silent. Then a deep feeling of sadness welled up within them both. As good Vikings they made no display of their grief, but when they covered their father over with a blanket, Leif said solemnly to his brother Thorvald, "Vinland the Good has brought us little luck. A tow boat full of timber and furs and vines is poor exchange for a good father."

Thorvald answered, "And it is likely to bring us even less luck before this plague has gone away.

Now I fear for our brother Thorstein, who is with the woman Gudrid in the byre."

Leif went quickly to the byre to fetch his brother away, but there he found that Thorstein had made up his mind to nurse the woman until she died. He had laid out a soft bed of hay for her and was bathing her face and arms with cool spring water to keep down her fever. When Leif came in, Thorstein said, "This woman has been crying out in her plague-dreams, brother. She is afraid that now that her husband Thorir is dead, she will travel alone forever through the darkness. It is pitiful to hear her."

Leif said, "I cannot change her bad dreams, brother. I am a Christian, not a spell-weaver. Our father Eirik has died, God rest his fierce soul, and I shall have all the weight of this settlement to bear, without meddling in what does not concern me."

Thorstein paled, and his eyes stared—first in disbelief, then in grief—into those of his brother. Soon he said, "I grieve for our father, but now that you are the chieftain at Brattahlid you must listen to all who come to you pleading. As you are a Christian and so is she, I beg you to marry us, here in this byre, so that Gudrid shall die with a quiet spirit."

So, with Thorvald as a witness, Leif married the two in the byre, sprinkling the stream water on both of them. After this, Gudrid fell into a deep sleep, with her hands crossed and a gentle smile upon her lips.

Then Leif and his brother went about the settlement, trying to bring what comfort they could to the
frightened folk, helping to carry bodies away from
the houses, and even to dig holes for them in Thjodhild's graveyard. These were shallow graves because
the ground was so hard.

Many times Leif called through the door of the
church to his mother, but she would not come out.
When he told her that Eirik had died, she only said,
"God rest his soul. He was a heathen man, but he
shall be buried in my churchyard all the same. That
much I will do for him. He was my husband."

Thorhall was there when she said this. He bit at
his beard with black fury and shouted, "Eirik did
not ask for Christ while he lived and you shall not
put this on him now that he cannot defend himself.
He shall have a proper burning, down on the fjord.
He shall go in the ship that brought him here. That
is his right as a Viking."

Now Leif put on his sternest face and said, "I am
the chieftain and the law-speaker, now that Eirik
has gone. And I say that he shall lie in the graveyard
as my mother wishes. I will listen to anything you
advise about sailing a ship or tracking a bear—but
you shall not tell me what to do with my own father.
Nay, do not frown and chew your beard at me,
Thorhall, I can swing an ax as well as you can. What
is more, I tell you this, that if it comes to ax-swing-

ing, when I have finished with you I shall put you in the churchyard too. So think on that."

Thorhall gave a loud bellow, clapped his hands over his ears, and ran away into the hills. No man saw him for three days.

At the end of that time Thorstein was dead too, but by some strange luck Gudrid was now as fresh and comely as she had ever been. All the plague-spots had gone from her. She came to Leif, who was mourning alone, and said, "Brother-in-law, I did not wish that good Thorstein should die in saving me. Will you ever forgive me?"

Leif gazed at her darkly for a while, his bearded chin on his hand as he sat in his father's chair. At last he said, "In this light, and standing as you do with your face toward the sunset, you remind me most strongly of a woman I met many years ago on an island of the Hebrides, when I was sailing to Norway for the first time. Her name was Thorgunna."

Gudrid looked at him in a puzzled way.

Leif watched her all the time, like a cat watching a mouse; then he said, "Now there is one question I must ask you. Will you answer it truthfully?"

Gudrid bowed her head and said, "I swear that I will answer whatever you ask, chieftain."

Then Leif said, "Are you a witch?"

Gudrid smiled sadly at this and shook her corn-golden head. "I am a Christian, Leif," she said. "We were all Christians on the ship. We prayed on that lonely reef for deliverance, and you came. Now, seeing what we have brought on you and your family, I wish that God had not answered our prayer. But perhaps He had a purpose in bringing us here. I do not know."

Leif glanced at her starkly and said, "Would you plunge both hands into a pot of boiling water and still say that you were not a witch? Would you take the test now?"

Gudrid looked down at her pretty white hands. Then she put them behind her back and said, "Yes, Leif, I will do that if you command it. Perhaps I owe Thorstein some suffering since he died for me. Let the kitchen-thralls bring in the boiling water."

Then Leif rose and went to her and put his arm about her shoulders and said, "I believe you, sister. Now I know that you are a true Christian. Have no fear of any more suffering. You are under my protection since you married my dead brother. I shall take you into my household and Thjodhild shall be as a mother to you too. One day, when all this mourning is over, I will find a good husband for you. So, Christ willing, in the end, good may come of this bad."

At last the plague passed and the settlement went about its living again. Eirik was buried in the graveyard, but one morning Leif walked there to find that an oak stake had been driven down into the soil where his heart would lie. He found Thorhall and said, "Why did you drive a stake through my father's heart, heathen?"

Thorhall looked away from him and said, "Did you see me do it? If you did not, then do not accuse me. But I will tell you that it is done to stop the dead from coming out of the ground again and frightening the living."

Leif said, "Eirik will never come out of the ground again. He has gone forever, and you must get used to that."

One evening Gudrid came to Leif in the hall and said, "Brother, I fell asleep beside Thorstein's grave in the churchyard this afternoon and he came to me in a dream. He was smiling and dressed in his blue feast robe with the white fox fur at the collar. His hair was combed and his beard curled as though for a great occasion. He was the most proper man I had seen."

Leif bowed his head and smiled. "There will be another proper man in your life, Gudrid," he said, "if you will have patience. Did our brother speak to you in this dream?"

She nodded and said, "He gave me stern advice, Leif, speaking with authority as though from a place where all the future was foretold. First he told me that I would have a great destiny, provided I never married another Greenlander. And second he told me that if this settlement were to prosper all heathen wickedness must be put down. He then commanded me to set my mind on gaining money for the Church, so that good priests should come out from Norway to this cold land."

Leif said, "And did you give him your promise, sister?"

Gudrid answered, "I did, Leif. I promised on my honor, and on my hope of Heaven."

Then Leif said, "Come, we will go to old Thjodhild and tell her this. She has little enough in her life now to be merry about. This could add years to her life."

And so they went to where Thjodhild was praying in her black gown. When they had told her of the dream, she wept for a while, then took Gudrid by the hands and said, smiling, "When you brought the plague here and stole my husband and my son from me, I wished you were dead on that lonely reef in the empty sea. But now I know that Christ was speaking through you and that our suffering was always meant to be. I have lost my kith and kin, but I have gained such a daughter as shall bring glory to the Church in Greenland. Together, my dear, we shall keep the Whitechrist alive in this wilderness. We shall stave off the black dream of disaster."

Leif saw the two women smiling into one another's eyes and, feeling like a child again in their presence, he bowed his head and went from the room.

Out on the green pasture he met his brother Thorvald, who was sitting on a stone and drawing with a twig in the hard soil. He said to Thorvald, "What are you doing, brother? You have made the shape of my longship, *Wolf-Snout*."

Thorvald looked up at him, the pale sunlight glinting on his short golden beard and in his clear blue eyes. He said, "Aye, brother, that I have. *Wolf-Snout* has been where I have never been. I have not seen the empty green sea and the lonely reefs. I have not set foot in Vinland the Good and seen the fat salmon in the clear blue lake there."

Leif sat down beside him and said, "There is much to be done in Greenland, brother. We have not conquered this cold stony place yet."

Then Thorvald got up from the stone and said, "That is your duty, now, chieftain. But mine is to see what Bjarni and you and Thorhall have seen."

Leif said, "Brother, I have only you left now. I cannot come with you to guide you. Is it wise to leave our mother with only one son?"

Thorvald said stiff-lipped, "She has Christ, chieftain. I have only a few years before my youth has gone. It is a man's duty to see the world God put him into. I shall go to Vinland in the spring. I would say the same to Red Eirik if he were here to listen to me."

Leif said, "Then who am I to deny you? My father was one of the few real men left in the world."

THORVALD'S VOYAGE

In the spring, with a wind running free toward the west, Leif went down to the fjordside to see his brother off. Thorvald had taken on a crew of thirty, many of whom had sailed with Leif, and they scoffed at the thought of danger on such a voyage. Thorhall went with the youngest of Eirik's sons and stood over him like a dark troll, snarling at all who came near him, even at Leif. Tyrkir the German did not go, but he had spent the winter months in carving the keel of the ship so that it should be more beautiful than any other to have sailed to the world's edge.

Thjodhild did not go to see Thorvald off; she said that she could do more good on her knees, praying for him in the church at Brattahlid. Gudrid kneeled beside her, in a dark gown, the memory of that lonely reef too much in her mind to let her wave farewell to others who might run upon it.

Leif said to Thorhall, grim faced like his father, "Take him there, and bring him back. That's all I ask. You may have the use of the huts I built by the lakeside, but never forget that they are mine. I am the chieftain in Vinland, just as I am in Greenland. Is that understood?"

Thorhall looked round, then bent and whispered to Leif, "Can you remember when I dangled you on my knee? Or when I taught you to walk and put my hand out to keep you from knocking your head on the tabletop?"

Leif said, "What are you trying to tell me, baresark?"

Thorhall said, "When you are older, you will know without being told. But in the meantime, you sit quietly here and take care of the women and their church. We men will tell you what happened when we get back."

Leif was very angry at this, but he was a chieftain now and had to hide his feelings, so he waved to the ship and wished it luck.

Yet it did not seem to need Leif's luck. *Wolf-Snout* was once more at anchor by the lakeside in Vinland, long before summer was drawing to its close. Thorvald laughed like a young boy as he

waded in the blue waters and learned from Thorhall how to catch salmon in his hands. They were
such sleepy fish, having lived under the sunshine
with no enemies for so long.

Thorvald said, "Leif reckons himself to be very
lucky, old Thorhall, and I grant you he is the chieftain in Greenland now that our father has gone into
the ground. I swear to obey him in all things, when
in Greenland, but here I feel that a true northman
has the right to look round and find himself a place
of his own. I would like my own settlement."

Thorhall smiled and said, "Who is arguing with
you, boy?"

So they took the ship's boat and two rowers and
went off down the coast, away from the pleasant
blue lake, and all the way found white sand beaches,
backed by thick and lush green woodlands.

Thorvald said, "This is indeed Paradise. How
could any man not be happy here? Why, old Thorhall, if men lived here they would never need to
shed blood, or even protect themselves, because God
has given enough for all to live on. I am amazed
that the world has gone on so long without this land
being found. The ways of God are indeed very
strange. To think that we, of all the men since Adam,
are the first to see this richness!"

Then, dead ahead, they sighted an island, pointed
in shape, with trees growing up to the summit and
white beaches all around it.

Thorvald said, pointing, "That is my place, old man. I am not ambitious like my brother Leif. I will settle for this little island. Here I will build the first house it has known and will fetch out a good wife from Greenland or Iceland, or even Norway. And here I shall live the gentle life I have always wanted. I shall not want to be a king or even a lord. I shall be content with being myself here. I know in my bones that I was meant to come out here and stay forever."

Thorhall did not answer him, but gave the rowers orders to put in at the first shallow landing they could find.

And so they did. And when they had beached the boat, they walked on the fine white sand dunes. But once they had gone over the first ridge, they stopped in silence, for there, nestling under the dark green woods, they saw a stockade of pointed sticks, as high as two men and lashed together as stoutly as any stockade they had ever seen.

Thorvald said at last, "I saw no other ships here. How could men be here?" He spoke in a low, shocked voice.

Thorhall answered, "Perhaps they have always been here and have not needed to come, as we have done, in ships. I am now so old that I am ready to believe anything."

Thorvald said, "Well, I have not come so far that I will tolerate any other man living here, unless he kneels to me as his overlord."

Thorhall smiled queerly and said, "Then let us go up and receive their homage. But, I beg you, keep your ax handy. You never know."

They went—Thorvald, Thorhall, and the two rowers—cautiously to the stockade, but no arrows flew at them. So, boldly they rattled on the fence and called for those inside to come out and talk. But no one came out.

And at last they sent one of the oarsmen over the top to see what was there. He came back and said that there was a house, of a strange sort, like nothing he had seen before, but no men and no trace of men, no cooking-pots or the white ashes of dead fires.

By this time the sun was setting and throwing its red glow across the woodland and waters. Thorvald felt a cold shiver run down his back. He turned to Thorhall and said softly, "I was mistaken, old one. This is not the place where I would choose to live alone with my family. Let us go back to Leif's huts by the lake while there is still light to see by."

All the way back they sat silent in that little boat, wondering who had set up the stockade. And that winter was as mild as the earlier one had been. The Greenlanders caught fish and gathered furs and timber, and once more built themselves a tow boat to take back all these things. Those who had not seen the little island with its deserted stockade were happy enough. The four who had wished they were already back in Greenland, cold and rocky though it was there.

At last, when the next spring came and the winds were right, they set off northward along the coasts, but after a week they were caught unaware by an inshore gust south of Markland and brushed against a hidden reef. *Wolf-Snout* groaned as though she were alive and Thorhall shouted out, "The keel has broken. We must put ashore and make a new one or we shall perish."

Thorvald was doubly angry because this keel had been carved specially for him by old Tyrkir. All the same, he accepted what had happened, and they got the longship ashore somehow and beached her out of the water's reach.

The men lost no time in chopping down the tall straight trees that lay just inshore, and in shaping them into a new keel to hold *Wolf-Snout's* strakes together. They wielded the axes well and there was little delay. Then Thorvald said to Thorhall, "My brother Leif never landed at this spot. He does not know everything, though he is the chieftain in Greenland. I will set my old keel up on this headland for all voyagers to see it in future times. They will say, 'Ah, there is Keelness, where Thorvald set up his carved wooden monument.' So, it could be that I shall be remembered even when Leif is forgotten."

Thorhall said dryly, "Aye, it could be. A man can only try."

When they had set up the keel with four feet of

earth around it to keep it steady against the sea winds, they sailed forth once more.

But two days onward, Thorvald said, "What have I done in my life that Leif has not done also, except set up a bit of carved wood on a headland? See, to our left hand lies a pretty white beach. I want to land there and build a few huts and call them mine. Then at least I shall come back from Vinland no worse than Leif did."

Thorhall said, "If you take my advice, you will keep straight on to the north till we get to gray Slabland and then turn east to Greenland."

Thorvald swung round on him and said, "Who do you think you are, heathen, to be giving advice to all and sundry? I have suffered you long enough."

Thorhall said, "Very well, let us land if you order it, master. You are old enough to choose your own doom."

And so they did. But behind a thick clump of salt grass they almost fell over three long birchbark canoes, with about nine men sleeping in their shelter. The Vikings drew back in horror at this and said, "These are trolls! Look at their black hair and their yellow faces. Look at the smallness of their arms and legs. And the thick stitching on their hide tunics! Oh, they are not human men as we are."

Thorvald said briefly, "Kill them and rid the world of such monsters."

The thirty Greenlanders rushed in with ax and

sword, and it was not hard work. Only one of the men woke and, picking up his light boat, ran away to the water and escaped, riding the water like a seal.

When it was all over, Thorvald said, "My mind is at rest now, Thorhall. These poor wizened creatures must have built that lonely stockade. If this is all we have to fear, then there is nothing to fear. For these poor little beasts are but Skraelings, or wretches, as one might call them."

Thorhall said, "We were thirty to eight, and that eight were sleeping. Suppose there were thirty such Skraelings, all awake, to face us. Would you still feel so victorious, Eirik's son? Would you dare face them?"

Now Thorvald was angry with the baresark and said, "Dare you go inland with me, toward that humped headland? I think that a fjord lies inland, beyond that hump, and there I shall live forever, Skraelings or not. Dare you come?"

Thorhall snorted down his nose and bushed his black beard out with his four fingers. "I dare do anything, boy," he said. "But you would be a wise child to go back into your ship and take shelter."

Thorvald glared at him and set off at a fast pace toward the hill. Thorhall ordered half the ship's company to stay aboard, ready to push out in a hurry if need be, and then led the others after Eirik's son. They caught up with him before he had reached the summit. And they all saw together that beyond the hill and all along the fjord was a great settlement of humped reed huts, much like beehives.

It took Thorvald long enough to understand that there were other men in the world than Green-landers. And then he said, "I beg your pardon, Thorhall. I am, as you say, a child."

The black baresark nodded and said smiling, "It takes a man to admit that he is a child. Now we had better get back to *Wolf-Snout* on our swiftest legs, because I can see a host of canoes coming out from the settlement to cut us off."

The Greenlanders ran like madmen and reached their longship in good time to defend it like a for-tress, but not in enough time to push it off into the tides.

Yet luck was with them, for only a few canoes came down to them, and they were more curious than furious. One of them paddled almost to within a spear's cast of *Wolf-Snout*, carrying four men, the first of whom wore a cloak and hood of rich furs, streaked in black and white.

Thorvald took him to be the chieftain of these folk, so he stood high on the prow-step and pointed with his spear. Then he called out, "I am a Christ-man, and no troll can harm me, monster. I tell you that your day has passed, so take warning. We shall soon come in our swarms."

Then he cast his iron spear, but he had misjudged

the range in that clear air, and the spear fell short, into the blue water. The chieftain in the striped furs watched it go down among the scattering fishes, then he turned and reached out his hand for his short bow and an arrow.

Thorvald saw him point the arrow. He even saw the red flint of its head for a moment in the sunlight. Thorhall said to him, "Jump down, you fool. Don't stand up there on the prow-step."

But Thorvald turned and said, "Would old Eirik have jumped down? Would Leif my brother? Would Thorstein even?"

When the blow came Thorvald turned to the baresark and shook his head, smiling starkly. He said, "I should have jumped down, old man. Now you will outlive me."

The chief in the black and white furs stood watching for a time. Then Thorvald felt under his left armpit and drew out the short arrow and showed it to him. The man nodded gravely from the distance and then turned his canoe away and left.

Thorhall caught Eirik's last son as he fell from the step. "Where shall we bury you, master?" he asked.

Thorvald whispered, "Back on that headland by my keel, south of Markland, heathen. And, I beg you, put crosses at my head and feet. I know it goes against your grain but, if I am to lie out here at the world's edge, I would like the best chance possible of getting to Heaven safely."

So they did this, even old Thorhall consenting, and then they went back to Greenland with all the tides and winds they needed, and were in Eiriks-fjord inside of two weeks.

When Leif heard of his brother's useless death, he struck Thorhall a hard blow on the right cheek. The baresark bowed beneath this blow but did not speak. He felt that he had deserved it.

And when Thjodhild heard the news of Thorvald's death, she turned to Gudrid and said gently, "How many men must a woman lose, so that a new world might be found? I have lost three now. There is only one left."

She staggered and seemed about to fall. Leif took her by the right arm and Gudrid by the left. Her son said, "Come, mother, we will go to your church and pray for little Thorvald's soul."

He thought he was doing the right thing. But when they had gone three paces, Gudrid whispered to him, "Do not drag at her any more, can you not feel that she is dead? Her heart has broken at the sad news."

Then Thorhall came up behind them and said, "I have always respected this great lady. Now give me leave to carry her to her church in my own arms. I am not a Christman and never shall be, but I am the only one of her own age living in this place now, and my master Eirik would have wanted me to take her where her heart belongs."

So the heathen carried Eirik's widow into her church and laid her dead body on the driftwood bier in the small nave. And when he came out again he paused by the door and said, "Whitechrist, I ask few favors. See that the old lady travels calmly to wherever you take them. I shall want a reckoning from you at the end of my day."

He shook his fist like a hammer at the altar and came out.

Leif met him and went with him behind the sheep byre and there used his blue wool chieftain's cloak to wipe the old baresark's cheeks dry of tears.

"I am grieved that I struck you, Thorhall," he said. "It was a thoughtless blow and one that I shall never be free of."

PART III

THE LAST SEEKERS

THORHALL'S SECOND WARNING 14

After the deaths of his mother and Thorvald, Leif seemed to age suddenly. He traveled on his roan horse through the settlements in Greenland, listened to all the people's problems, and tried to make peace among them when feuds began. When the Greenlanders held their Thing assembly, Leif saw that justice was done fairly to all. At other times he watched the unloading of cargoes from Iceland and Norway and saw that the foreign merchants did not cheat the Greenlanders or the Greenlanders the merchants. He organized a coastal patrol of ships, whose duty it was to see that the seas around the southern tip of Greenland were clear of pirates.

He even tried to like Freydis, his sullen sister, and

her weak-willed husband, though this was more difficult than sweeping the pirates away. Whatever Leif said, Freydis was bound to take the opposite view. She seemed determined to quarrel with everyone she met. It was as though she could not help herself. And always her husband, Thorvard of Gardar, sided with her, however wrong she was.

One evening, sitting by the fire, Leif said to old Thorhall, "Freydis will bring dishonor on the name of our family, mark my words, friend. If only her husband would control her, she might turn out to be a good woman in the end. She is shrewd enough at housekeeping and farming."

Thorhall said gruffly, "Her husband could not control a sheep, much less such a wolf of a woman. I would never turn my back on such a woman if she had a knife in her hand."

Leif smiled and said, "There, there, baresark—she is not as bad as that. She may be spiteful and bitter and sharp tongued, but she is not a murderess."

Thorhall said, "She may not have struck the blow yet, lad, but she has it in her heart. I shall say no more. But watch her, that is my advice to you."

Leif said very gravely, as a chieftain should, "You cannot make such accusations, Thorhall, without something to back them up. What is on your mind? Come on, speak out, I must hear."

Thorhall said, "Your mother and father are dead.

Your two brothers are dead. You and Freydis are the only two of old Eirik's blood left. Being the eldest son, you hold Eirik's land and all his livestock. Freydis has nothing, except what her husband has. Suppose you were to die, by falling over a cliff, or drowning in the fjord, or drinking a cup of poisoned ale. . . . What would happen then, Leif?"

Leif said, "All my belongings would go to Freydis, of course. That is the law. She is next of kin."

Thorhall nodded. "She might help you to die, chieftain, so that she could get the land and cattle, and her husband could become the greatest man in Greenland, don't you think?"

Leif said slowly, "You are not as mad as I thought, old one. I will watch her, as you say."

Thorhall said then, "There is one other way to stop her gallop. If you were to marry a good woman and raise a family of your own, then your children would inherit the land and livestock. She could not kill them all."

Leif frowned and said, "What you advise is no doubt true enough, but I am not the sort of man who cares much for marriage. I like to run my house as I please, and I do not wish to be ruled by a wife. Nor am I cut out to be a kind father. I have so many things to attend to in the settlement, there is little time for playing with children. Besides, I am happy enough as I am, with all my servants and thralls to attend to things for me."

Thorhall said, "Why do you not marry Gudrid? She is a fine woman and knows your habits. She would not try to rule you. Indeed, for a Christian, she is quite outstanding. If all Christians were like Gudrid, I might even become one myself."

Leif answered, "I cannot marry Gudrid, even if she would have me, because that would go against the wishes of my dead brother Thorstein, who warned her in a dream never to marry another Greenlander. I would not wish to bring her doom upon her, Thorhall."

The Hunter glowered at him darkly, then said, "Well, there is only one other way in which you can keep Freydis from getting her claws on your farmstead, short of throwing her into the fjord with a stone tied to her ankles—which, as a good Christian, you could never bring yourself to do."

Leif looked up sharply. "And what is that way, Thorhall?" he asked.

But the old man was now weary of the talk and shrugged his shoulders. "If you don't know, then I shall not tell you," he said. "The folk here come to you for your wise advice—use some of it for yourself, if you are so clever."

THE MAN ON THE ROCK 15

After his conversation with Leif, Thorhall stomped off down to the fjord, where he had a comrade called Bjarni Grimolfsson, an Icelander from Breidafjord, who was a great rover and a fierce fighter, much like Thorhall himself. This Bjarni always stayed just within the law, though there were many farmers in the settlement who thought they saw their sheep grazing in his pens. Only Leif and Thorhall could deal with him; all other Greenlanders backed away from his fierce scowling and his restless right hand.

He said to Thorhall, "Did you warn Leif about his sister?"

Thorhall nodded. "He will not take advice," he said.

Bjarni laughed. "If he would only whisper the word to me," he growled, "I would attend to the matter. Of course, I should want Thorvard's farmstead in payment, but Leif has enough as it is. He does not need any more land to look after."

Thorhall frowned and said, "It is a good thing that you have said this to me and not to anyone else. Murder is a very serious thing."

Bjarni laughed and said, "Oh, I know you are safe enough, old baresark. You would never tell Leif what I have said. I know too much about a few things that you have done in the past, don't I?"

Thorhall regarded him stiffly for a while and fingered the hilt of his iron knife. Then he let his hand fall and nodded. "Aye," he said. "Friends we are, and friends we must stay. We have been in a few scrapes together that would not sound very well if they were laid before the Thing assembly for judgment."

Bjarni clapped him on the shoulder and said, "Come, Thorhall, I have had enough of this. Let us take my ship down the fjord to see if the waves have washed anything up lately. I need some driftwood for a fence."

They swept away down the blue water, but soon, lying with its back broken across a saw-toothed reef, they saw a small ship with one man clinging to it and shouting. As they drew closer, Bjarni said, "That ship never came from Iceland or Norway. And it is not an English pirate, either. What can it be?"

Thorhall stood in the prow listening to the voice of the man shouting out at them. He said to Bjarni, "I have heard that tongue before. They speak it in the Hebrides."

Bjarni said, "Well, I do not feel like risking my ship to run in close on that reef to rescue a Hebridean. If it were an Icelander, I might take the chance. But not for a red-shanked fellow who yaps in the language of sea gulls and seals."

Thorhall said, "Hey, hold the ship steady. Can't you see, this loon wears a gold ring round his throat and bracelets on both arms. He is no common fisherman, friend. He must be a prince, or at least a lord. We might do well to put in to the reef and haul him off."

Bjarni nodded. "At least we can take a look at him. We can always knock him on the head and pitch him overboard when we have had a better look at the gold he wears."

As they drew nearer Bjarni said, "Thor! But look at the ship he sailed in. It is nothing more than tarry hides spread over a long basket of willow wands. To have come so far in such a cockleshell!"

Thorhall nodded grimly. "I know these folk," he said. "They are not brave in the way we are, but they are a very old people who know some things that we of the north have not yet learned about sailing."

Bjarni scoffed and said, "Well, he has not learned to keep afloat as far as land, anyway."

"No," said Thorhall thoughtfully, "but he has learned enough to fetch us down the fjord to pick him up, and that was no easy thing."

They saw that the young man had dark brown hair with red glints in it like bronze. He was very pale faced and had strange green eyes. At first he was hissing like a wild cat, but as they stood off at oar's length he called out to them in good Norse, "Throw me a rope and pull me in. Make haste, my fingers are giving way."

Bjarni said to Thorhall, "He commands us as though we were thralls. I have half a mind to pull away and leave him to the sea."

But Thorhall shook his head. "Do as he asks," he said. "I have a feeling that it will be better that way."

The stranger caught the rope they flung and then jumped aboard as spry as a lark. The first thing he did was to draw his long iron dirk from his leather belt and to wipe its blade carefully on a sheepskin that lay aboard. It was a black-looking weapon with a vicious edge. When he had done this he looked at Bjarni and said, "Take me to Leif Eiriksson now."

While Bjarni gasped at the young man's pride,

Thorhall said, "Are you sure that Leif will want to see you, Redshanks?"

The young man snarled a little at him, then said, "It will be best for him if he does. I think he has been waiting for me these many years. Turn your ship round and set course. I am cold and hungry. I am not used to being kept waiting."

Then he went to the aftercabin and made himself comfortable on Bjarni's thong chair without asking the shipmaster's leave. Bjarni was about to go for him, but Thorhall drew him back and whispered, "Steady, old mate. Do not start something you cannot finish. It is my guess that this lad knows how to use that pig-sticker of his, and you have left your ax at home."

Bjarni said starkly, "Very well, there's always tomorrow."

He spoke in a very low voice and the wind was whistling round him, but the youth with green cat's eyes suddenly looked up and said, "There may not be tomorrow for certain folk, unless they learn better manners."

And when they put ashore below Brattahlid, the young man leaped like a stag onto dry land and strode up the hill toward the steading without asking the way.

Bjarni said, "I do not like the look of this at all, Thorhall. Nay, I do not care for it."

Thorhall nodded. "No more do I," he said. "It is my place to hurry after him and to see that no harm befalls Leif."

He ran up the slope after the long-shadowed youth, and was amazed when the Hebridean halted and stood waiting for him, his pale face set and glowering. He called to Thorhall, "Whose dog are you, Blackbeard? Are you in such a hurry to be whipped?"

Thorhall bit his lip, then said, "There is no man in Greenland who dares say that to me."

The youth said, "Then the times have changed, Blackbeard, because there is now a man in Greenland who dares say anything to anyone. Throw that dagger of yours into the grass, or I shall step down the hill and put you to certain trouble. I do not carry this dirk for skinning rabbits."

Thorhall thought that his head would burst, the blood beat so hard in his temples. Then suddenly he began to laugh and then flung his dagger away where he could find it again. He said, "I think I remember you now. Or, at least, not you, but one like you."

The youth nodded and said without smiling, "I do not remember you, but I know who you are. And Leif will know who I am. Now walk before me where I can keep my eye on you, and take me straight to Eiriksson. If you try any Norse tricks, I

shall have the ugly head off your thick shoulders before you can draw three breaths."

Thorhall shook his head. "I must say, you are a
proper man," he said. "If I could get close to you,
I could break you in two pieces with my bare hands.
But you are every inch a man."

The youth said coldly, "What did you expect me
to be, a mouse like Thorvard of Gardar?"

This shook Thorhall so much, he did not say another word until they both stood before Leif in the
hall at Brattahlid.

Then he said, "Master, I bring you a visitor."

The youth said, "Save your breath, Blackbeard.
He has been expecting me for half his life."

Leif gazed into the young man's eyes, then said
to Thorhall, "Sit by the fire, old friend. We shall say
nothing that you may not hear too."

Then Leif placed his hands on the youth's
shoulders and drew him to his breast, as a father
does to a son who has been away for many years.
Tears were running down his cheeks, and Thorhall
had never seen this happen before, not even when
Eirik the Red died.

Then Leif said, "How is your mother, boy? I have
dreamed of her for years, especially since the misfortune came on my family."

The young man said, "She died two months ago.
But on her deathbed she commanded me to return

the gold ring and the ivory belt you once gave her as a betrothal present. She could not return the green cloak because she wished to be buried in it."

He felt in his pouch and laid the ring and belt upon Leif's chair. Then he said, "My mother, Thorgunna, Lady of the Islands, gave me the name Thorgils. She forgave you for not keeping your promise to return and marry her, but she put a gentle spell on you to make sure that you married no one else."

Leif nodded and smiled. "Aye, I know it," he said. "And you, Thorgils, are the son I should have had if I had kept my promise, are you not? You are the son of my dreams."

The youth nodded and then bowed before Leif. He said, "I am the son of your dreams, come now to take care of you for the rest of your days."

Thorhall by the fire stood and said, "Somehow I knew you the moment you turned on me, above the fjord, Master. I felt the magic come out of your eyes into my stomach and turn it as cold as ice."

Thorgils laughed for the first time then and said, "It took all the strength from me to lay that spell on you, baresark. I am truly glad that you did not come on at me then. I should have finished you, of course, but it would have left me very weak."

Thorhall came forward and took the young man's hand and pressed it to his cheek. It was a very cold hand, but very strong. Thorhall said, "Tell me, Thorgils Leifsson, how many good men did you lose, bringing your crazy tarred boat all the way from the Hebrides?"

Thorgils smiled thinly at him then and said, "None, old warrior. I came alone. I brought my mother's thong and made the wind-knots in it to guide me. That is all."

Thorhall said slyly, "But you have no spells to deal with our Greenland reefs, is that it?"

Thorgils smiled again, and it was like the ice breaking in the spring. He said, "I put the boat onto the reef after some thought. If I had sailed it up the fjord unaided, the good folk at Eiriksfjord would have stoned me to death. It was better to come in as a wrecked rover. You simple folk are used to that. You welcome wrecked seafarers."

Then Thorhall began to laugh and to slap his thigh. But Leif stopped him and said gravely, "You see now why I did not marry in order to have an heir to the steading, Hunter? And you see why I have not married Gudrid off already? This is the right husband for her. He is not a Greenlander, and together they can take over Brattahlid when I am gone and keep Freydis in her place. Fetch Gudrid straightway, Thorhall. These two must meet."

But when Gudrid came in, dressed in her green robes and wearing a necklace of jet, she shrank a little from Thorgils' touch. And after a time she excused herself, saying that she felt very cold and must go to her fireside in the bower to get warm again.

When she had gone, Leif asked, "What was it, my son?"

Thorgils smiled sadly and answered, "It cannot be, father. She is a true Christian. Did you not see how she drew away from the ancient magic in me?"

Leif said, "I am a Christian too, my son. Did you not know?"

Thorgils nodded, then said, "Aye, father, but your religion is like well-watered voyage-ale, it is not all that strong. We shall get on very well together, I can tell. But Gudrid is not the wife for me, you must find someone else for her."

Word soon went out that Leif had adopted a son to take over Brattahlid when his days were ended, and it was not long before Freydis and her rabbit-toothed husband Thorvard of Gardar came hurrying to find out what this son was like.

When Freydis saw Thorgils in his green kilt and red cloak, with the gold at his throat and arms, and his great dirk stuck proudly in his belt, she could not help smiling sweetly and making eyes at him. And the more coldly he treated her, the more she tried to catch his attention. At last, she said aloud to her husband, "If you were more like this Hebridean I should be content."

Thorvard was very angry at this and stalked over

to Thorgils and glared at him. "You may carry a dirk in your belt, boy," he said, "but do you know how to use it?"

Everyone in the hall was silent then. Thorhall bowed his head so that no one should see him smiling.

But Thorgils only stared palely and said in a gentle voice, "Aye, Rabbit-teeth, I know how to use it."

Then he stood quite still, like a block of ice, and did not say another word. Thorvard gasped as though he had fallen into the fjord, and then did not know how to go on. He gaped for a time, trying to get his breath, then he turned round and almost rushed out of the hall.

Freydis went after him, and the folk in the hall heard the sound of many hard thumps before she came in again, red faced and with her hair in dis-array. She went straight to Thorgils and said, "I must ask you to pardon my husband, brother. As you see, he is a man of violent temper. It is all I can do to stop him from going wild at times."

Thorgils bowed and said, "You have my sym-pathy, lady. He is the sort of man I should not wish to offend."

There was another stiff silence and she shuffled from foot to foot, until at last she too made her way quickly from the hall. And when the folk had all gone, Leif said to Thorgils, "Old Eirik is dead, but there is a man in Greenland again. You will keep them all in order, my son."

Thorgils said, "Thank you, father. I shall always do as you wish me to do. I shall care for you as my mother would have done. That is why she dreamed me, to give peace to your life in these times of trouble."

After that, no more was said. They were the happiest father and son in the North.

KARLSEFNI

When Freydis found that Leif was beyond her reach and that Thorgils was like a calm and steadfast watchdog that could not be bribed with a bone to let the thieves come in, she turned her attention toward Gudrid and made her life a misery.

At last Thorhall went to Leif and said, "Master, Gudrid is either weeping or praying all the time now, and that is no way for a young woman to live her life."

Leif answered, "I would to God I could find her a husband to protect her, but I have considered all the families I remember in Iceland, and I cannot think of anyone there who could stand up to this vixen, Freydis."

Thorgils was polishing a bronze brooch by the hearth and paused in his work to look up and say, "Rack your brains no further, Leif. A ship from Norway is rounding Cape Farewell now, with a stout east wind in the sail. It will bring good news to you and to Gudrid."

Leif put down his cup and stared at the young man. "Tell me the name of the shipmaster," he said, smiling bleakly.

Thorgils answered, "I do not play at silly games, father. The power I have is not to be used like that. All I will tell you, since you seem to be in some doubt, is that he will wear a sheepskin dyed red, and that the top of his right forefinger is missing. Will that do?"

Then he bent over the brooch again, without waiting for Leif's reply. And at sunset, two days later, a great black-painted trading ship pulled into the haven at Eiriksfjord. When the plank was set down, a man wearing a red sheepskin jacket and holding a black staff in his maimed right hand stepped ashore. He looked round smiling for a while, then said to Thorhall, who was there to meet him, "I am the Norwegian, Karlsefni. I come to visit Leif Eiriksson and to trade with him."

Thorhall bowed his head slightly and said smiling back, "We were expecting you. Will you follow me up to the house?"

Karlsefni nodded pleasantly and said, "Leif must have good spies out. We only rounded Cape Farewell two days ago, with an east wind in the sail."

Thorhall said gently, "We who live up here come to know all the winds and the tides. We can judge how long it will take a ship to get up the fjord, more or less."

Karlsefni scratched the side of his fine nose and said, "It is good to be among such sharp seafarers. The old spirit has died out in Norway, I fear. And soon it will be gone in Iceland. As for the English, they never had it; with them it was only a dream. But, up here, a man can find sea rovers still, I think. Men who would sail to the world's edge."

Thorhall coughed slightly at this and Karlsefni said, "I do not suppose that you have been to this Vinland they are all talking about in Bergen and Bremen?"

Thorhall shrugged his shoulders. "Only twice," he said. "Mind that hole in the ground, master, you could fall into it with all that hay lying over it. I must get it filled in before the winter makes the ground too hard to dig."

Karlsefni gazed at him in astonishment and did not say another word all the way up to Brattahlid. There Leif greeted him well and said, "I am glad that you have come, with such a great store of provisions too. Here in the settlement we expected to go hungry before the winter was out. Our harvests have not been good, and the nets have not brought in many fish."

At that moment Gudrid came into the hall, dressed in a new linen robe and wearing the best of her ornaments. It was plain to all who saw this meeting that Karlsefni could not take his eyes off her.

And late that evening he said in private to Leif, "Lord, I am not one who makes up his mind lightly, and when I ask for a thing I mean that I want that thing above all others. I have good holdings in Norway and am well respected there."

Leif nodded and smiled. "I know what you are going to ask," he said. "What do you think the lady concerned will say?"

Karlsefni said, "I think that she would listen to my proposal. Have I your permission to ask her?"

Leif said, "I will come with you to her bower, so that all may be done properly in our Greenland way."

The outcome was that the two were married by Leif in due course, and the wedding feast was the best the settlers had ever known. Karlsefni had brought great stores of malt, grain, and flour, which he shared generously with all who came to the feasting. The celebrations went on long after Christmas, and there was much singing and chess-playing and storytelling. Even Freydis so far forgot herself as to sing in the hall before the folk, though a quarrel almost arose there because she could not keep her eyes off Thorgils as she sang, and this angered her husband, Thorvard of Gardar—especially since he could do nothing about it.

Karlsefni turned this quarrel aside by asking for news of Vinland, and all who had been there had something to say. When the story had been told, Karlsefni said, "This is the land of heart's desire. With my new wife, I would be happy to settle in Vinland for the rest of my days. Have I your permission, Leif, to take as many of the Greenlanders as wish to come with me, and to form a new settlement there?"

Leif said, "They are all free folk here, brother-in-law. They can decide for themselves. I would not want the farms here to suffer from not having enough folk to tend them, but no one can force a man to stay if he wishes to go somewhere else."

Freydis jumped up then and said, "Why am I always left out of things? If Gudrid goes to Vinland, I too shall go. I see no reason why my husband Thorvard should not start his settlement there too, if this Norwegian is allowed to."

Leif said, "No one is denying you, Freydis."

Indeed, he was glad that she wished to go from Greenland. Then she said, "And while we are at it, you cannot leave Brattahlid, now that you are the chieftain here, so you will not need those houses you built beside the lake in Vinland. As your sister, I shall claim them before this stranger does."

Now Leif's face grew very red and he clenched his fist about his meat knife. He said firmly for all to hear, "Those huts are mine, Freydis, and shall never belong to any other man. If you want houses in Vinland, then you must build them yourself. In the meantime, I will gladly give you permission to live in them until your own are made. And you shall share them equally with Karlsefni and his folk. That is my word."

Thorhall was drinking ale with his mate Bjarni in a corner by the wood-stove. He said with a grim smile, "That woman will be the death of many men, my friend, before all is over. See, she promises gaily enough now, but once she is beyond Leif's reach, see how she will change."

Bjarni laughed quietly and said, "We are not boys, old one. We can fend for ourselves, hey? She will not bring the doom on us, will she?"

Thorhall said, "When my doom comes, it will come from something stronger than a red-haired woman with a whiplash for a tongue."

Just as he spoke a spark flew from the stove into his beard, and set it smoldering. Bjarni laughed to see him beating the fire out, and said, "That is an omen of some sort, but what it means I do not know."

Karlsefni watched this and said to Leif, "That is

a strange man, that black baresark who sets his beard on fire. I am not sure that I would want to take him to Vinland."

Leif said, "He is a strange man, to be sure, but my dead father put his trust in him and so must you. He knows every rock and inlet between here and my huts in Vinland. He can find food when an eagle can see nothing to eat. This Thorhall could make or break your expedition, however well you plan it."

Karlsefni said quietly, "But he is a heathen, is he not?"

Leif nodded. "Aye, a heathen," he said. "And so was my father—but he founded Greenland, all the same. It does not seem to me that Christ is a better voyager than old Redbeard Thor. I have heard some seafarers say that they pray to the one on land and to the other at sea. Perhaps you should do the same, brother-in-law, on this venture of yours."

Then he laughed and called for more meat and bread. Karlsefni went to his wife Gudrid and said, "I am not sure that Leif is as good a Christian as folk make out."

She smiled and answered, "He is good enough for me, husband, and so he must be good enough for you." So Karlsefni said no more.

THE GREAT SAILING **17**

When spring came, the great sailing began. There had been no other expedition like it from Greenland. Leif and Thorgils watched from the fjord slope as the longships went out, each with its tow boat trailing behind on the level waters. Sheep and cattle cried out mournfully, their voices echoing weirdly along the fjord. From one barge came the deep throated bellowing of a bull.

Leif said, "That is Karlsefni's beast. It knows no master. That bull would try to overthrow a great church, if it stood in his way."

Thorgils smiled. "That is what it will do, father," he said. "That bull will ruin a land. It will set the world back for twenty generations."

Leif turned to him and said sternly, "Come, come, lad. I spoke only in a sort of joking. No beast could do what I said, and what you said still less."

Thorgils said, "I shall not answer you. You must look down from the Heaven you pray for and see what I mean, a long time hence."

Leif turned from him in annoyance and watched the ships. Karlsefni led with three vessels, long red cloths floating at the masthead, and beside him sailed Freydis, with two more ships steered by the brothers Helgi and Finnbogi. Thorhall came behind, in a longship that Thorbjorn Vifilsson had brought from Iceland. Alongside Thorhall rode his old mate Bjarni Grimolfsson in his own craft. Karlsefni's own party was of sixty men and five women, but all told the expedition numbered one hundred and sixty, including a number of husbandless girls. Leif had not thought it wise to take these women, fearing that quarrels would break out among shipmen because of them. But Freydis was stanch on this and said, "These girls must live somewhere. If their parents sail to Vinland, leaving them behind, will you take on the duty of feeding them, clothing them, finding them husbands, and then paying for their wedding feasts?"

So Leif gave in; a man would need to have the Treasure of Miklagard in his coffers to stand against that woman's argument. And when this noisy company had sailed down the fjord and had gone round the wooded headland to be hidden from view, and when the horn-blowing, and singing, and bleating of sheep, and lowing of cattle, and bellowing of bulls, and clucking of hens had faded over the glassy water, Leif turned to Thorgils and said, "Well, son, that is the beginning of Vinland—and the end of Greenland."

Thorgils said, "You are only half right, Leif."

Leif searched him hard with his eyes and asked, "Which half is right, then?"

But Thorgils only said, "Why are you not content to let life flow about you, like water from a stream? Why must you always be turning rivers out of their courses? Why must you want to know on which day you will die? Does such knowledge make a man happier? Was it not better for old Eirik's father to die by surprise, alone in the dark byre?"

Now Leif had never mentioned his grandfather Thorvald before, and when Thorgils said this he felt a strange lifting of the hair on his neck as though a chilly blast had swept over him, and he said in a small voice, "I think I am afraid of you, my son. I think you know more than a man should."

Thorgils picked up a flat stone and tried to skim it across the waters of the fjord, but it fell short and did not reach the water. He turned to Leif and shrugged his shoulders, smiling. "See," he said, "but you could get a stone to skim halfway across that little stream."

So Leif went up to the steading with him, less afraid now. And by-and-by they got about the work of hay-harvesting, then corn-harvesting, then ale-brewing, then beast-salting, then deer-hunting, then gathering driftwood against the winter snows.

And while they were at all this, the expedition went on and on. As Karlsefni saw it, guided through gentle weather by so many seafarers of experience, it was hardly more than sailing round the lip of a huge bowl of gray rock. He wondered now why the men in Norway made such a terrifying mystery of this journey. To Gudrid he said, "Why, wife, it is only patience that is needed. Patience, and more patience, and still more. A man does not need even courage—only patience and the right winds."

They had just passed the reef where she had been wrecked. She nodded and said, "Yes, husband. Just patience. What else is there in life?"

THE QUARRELS BEGIN **18**

Two days from starting the voyagers sighted Slab-land, with its glaciers and great flat rocks lapped by the sea and white foxes scurrying here and there after grouse and hares. Thorhall said, "If I were among that lot I'd bring back a feast robe before you could count a hundred."

In two more days, with a fierce wind behind them, they sighted the green woods of the next place, which was Markland. Once more they went southward and in two days saw the headland at Keelness, where Thorvald's keel stood against the sky, bleak and lonely. Freydis said, "My brother picked a decent enough place to be buried. It's a pity Leif doesn't come out and join him in the ground." Her voice was like sour wine.

Then they went tacking along the white coast and soon ran past many bays and little fjords, into one of which Karlsefni drew the ships. And here the settlers camped for a while until Karlsefni was certain of their position. Thorhall told him to go on south a while to find Vinland, but Karlsefni stared at him coldly and said, "You may have been there before, man, but your memory may have failed. I want to be certain of all things before I put my peoples' lives in danger. I am a trader, not a hero."

So he sent the two Scots, Haki and Hekje, to run southward overland and bring back news of what they found. At the end of three days these swift runners came smiling and carrying grapes and wheat in their shoulder bags. Thorhall said, "Did I not tell you so, Norwegian?"

Karlsefni nodded. "You did," he said, "but as I told you, I am a merchant by trade and in many dealings I have learned not to trust everything I hear."

Thorhall flared at this and shouted, "Do you call me a liar? Eirik never called me a liar."

Karlsefni turned away from him and said, "I cannot waste my time on every madman who wishes to quarrel with me. Let us set off again, toward the south, where Vinland lies."

But Thorhall ran at him and swung him round by the arm. He said, "Now you have called me a liar and a madman. All the folk have heard you belittle me. This is your first mistake and I shall not forgive you until I have my revenge."

The girls giggled at this, but the men glared at them until they were silent, for it was a serious matter when leaders insulted one another and vowed vengeance. Helgi said in a whisper to Finnbogi, "If we were wise, we would turn back now, the two of us, before winter comes on and the seas are impassable. I feel that no good will come of this voyage."

Freydis came up behind them and said, "What are you two whispering about?"

Helgi turned on her coldly and said, "Something that does not concern you, woman. You may be able to rule your little husband, but we are a different sort of beast—you cannot rule us."

Freydis glared at him and bit her lip. "We shall see about that," she said. "I shall remind you of this moment at a later time, never fear." Then she strode away to her own ship.

Finnbogi said, "We cannot turn back now, friend, or she will boast that she has frightened us, and our name as stout men will be lost. We must go on with the others, and hope to be given the chance of putting this wicked woman in her place before long."

Unrest spread among the voyagers, but when they saw the place they were to live in, they forgot the quarrels and could not wait to land. They passed the little island at the mouth of the fjord and saw that it was so crowded with eider duck that a man could not set his foot down anywhere without breaking eggs. And all along the fjord the green grass grew so lush that the cattle in the tow boats smelled it and cried out to be set ashore to graze.

Karlsefni laughed at them and said, "Wait, wait, little brothers, soon you shall feast until you are as fat as butter. I have never seen such good grazing in my life."

Before long they came to the blue lake and saw Leif's houses standing by the shore, looking as inviting as when they were first built. Soon Freydis went to Karlsefni and claimed half of the huts for her people to live in. He answered, "You have fewer folk than I have to look after. So you need fewer houses."

Freydis took hold of his belt and would not let it go. "Leif is my brother," she said. "But you have no blood tie with him. That gives me greater rights than you, Norwegian."

He could see that she was set on having her own way, and he did not wish to quarrel again, fearing it might come to blows. He saw that Thorhall had sided with Freydis already—though Helgi and

Finnbogi, her two captains, stood away from her, frowning. Karlsefni said to Freydis, "My wife Gudrid hopes to have her baby in the spring. I want that child to be born into a peaceful world, so I shall not quarrel with you."

Then Freydis said fiercely, "And I also hope to have a baby in the spring, and I do not care whether it is born into a peaceful world or not. My child will fight its way through life, Karlsefni, and will not grow up idle, to live off the labor of other people. I shall have the houses, not because you give them but because I take them."

Then she let go his belt and he shrugged his shoulders. So that quarrel passed and Karlsefni set men on to chop down trees and lay the timber on the rocks to season in the sunshine. It was no great hardship to build other houses.

Meanwhile, the sheep and cattle and pigs fed to their heart's content. As for the settlers, they found grapes and game in profusion and hardly had to walk a hundred paces to knock down a plump deer with an arrow.

Thorhall glowered at Bjarni and said, "This sort of life ruins a hunter. Everything comes too easily."

Bjarni said smiling, "It suits me, brother. I live only for today. Tomorrow can take care of itself."

Most of the settlers felt the same. They thought that summer would last forever and so they made little effort to gather stocks of food.

Now one day Karlsefni was walking along the fjord with Gudrid when suddenly she shuddered and said, "The wind has changed, husband. It blows from the north not the east and there are ice arrows in it."

He smiled and said, "Wrap your cloak round you. You are dreaming."

But as he spoke the broad blue sky vanished as though a great gray hand had snatched it away, and without any warning swift scurries of snowflakes howled about them. By the time they had struggled back to their house, the settlement lay under a white blanket and the snow kept coming. Men shivered by small fires, since they had not thought to get wood chopped; and the cattle stood knee-deep in drifts, bewildered that the green pasture had been taken away from them so suddenly.

This was only the beginning. By the end of a month of such blizzards, the settlers cursed the day they ever set eyes on Vinland. Now Thorhall went boldly to Karlsefni and said, "Merchant, listen to a hunter. If you want to keep these people alive through this winter, divide the men into two companies. While one company is out hunting by daylight for food, let the other chop down as many saplings as it can, and set up a firm stockade round this village. Soon the wolves will come, and then we shall be the hunted not the hunters."

Karlsefni did this, though with a bad grace, and

when the stockade was up, he had all the cattle driven into it. After that, the wolves came every night and scratched and howled outside, trying to get in. Now the days grew very short and there was little enough time in which to hunt. The wheat and vines had all shriveled. Often the folk had to satisfy their hunger by chewing at pieces of old hide. Some of them ate bark from the stockade posts. The ground was now so hard that the old ones who died could not be buried but were propped by the stockade under a covering of snow.

When things were at their worst, Thorhall went off one day and did not return. On the next day Bjarni went to Karlsefni and told him. The two went out into the icy wind and searched for him, and at the end of the day they found him on the top of a cliff, his shirt wide open, his eyes turned back in his head, his face a mottled red. He was praying in a strange language. They had to carry him back to the settlement, he was so stiff-legged and frozen. Then Karlsefni said to him, "What were you doing there? Why did you put us into such danger, searching for you?"

Thorhall said, "What I was doing, you will soon find out. As for danger, I was getting you out of it, not into it. See that the young men search the coast by the mouth of the fjord early tomorrow." Then he would say no more, but fell into a deep sleep.

The next morning, the young men came rushing back to say that they had found a whale stranded on the shore. All the settlers ran down with axes and knives and staggered home late in the day loaded with meat for the cooks to boil in their iron cauldrons. That evening there was great feasting inside the stockade.

But the following day all the folk save Thorhall were sick and it was not long before Karlsefni went to the baresark and said, "I do not like this. There was something wrong with that whale meat. The folk cannot keep it down. Now they are in a worse state than ever."

Thorhall laughed up at him and said, "They will keep it down well enough, as I have done, if they will only give thanks to Thor, who sent it to them."

At this Karlsefni almost ran from Thorhall's hut and, gathering the folk, told them that they had been tricked into eating heathen food. They followed him painfully up to the cliff top where Thorhall had been found, and they flung what was left of the meat into the sea.

After that, all the folk of the settlement knelt and prayed to Christ for help. The whale meat seemed to boil for a while in the sea, then vanished as though a great hand had dragged it down from below. And when these people went back to the settlement they found a herd of caribou grubbing in the snow nearby, so intent on what they were doing that they did not hear the hunters string their bows and let drive their arrows.

That day the weather broke for a time, and the men were able to bring fish in from the fjord. Thorhall lay on his bed and bit the coverlet in fury.

ONE QUARREL ENDS 19

Before that winter passed a terrible thing happened in the settlement. A sort of madness came over Freydis and she did everything she could to annoy Helgi and Finnbogi. First she turned them out of their huts and forced them to build others, though the cold was bitter; then she began to threaten them, saying that she wanted their ships and would have them flung out of the village into the snow unless they gave them up to her.

The two brothers were ashamed to tell Karlsefni what was going on, and they did not deign to tell Thorvard, her husband, a man they despised. Then, after this had been going on for weeks, one morning before dawn Freydis appeared in their huts dressed only in her nightshift, and said, "Let us be friends at last. Look, I need a bigger ship than the one I have. Will you exchange yours for mine, Finn-bogi? I ask no more."

He was so weary with all this bickering, he sat up in bed and said, "Yes, lady, I will agree to that. I cannot stand this quarrel one moment longer. It is no way for settlers to live."

Freydis smiled and said, "Now you will not have to stand it any longer. Now you shall soon see what sort of friend I can be."

So she went away and the brothers lay back to sleep again, thankful that at last they could live in peace. On her way home, Freydis made sure that her gown was wet through in the snow and that her bare feet were as cold as ice. Once inside her house she woke Thorvard up and began to scream out, "See what they have done to me, those brothers. They dragged me outside while you snored, and have thrashed me like a slave. I do not think I shall live after such treatment." Her hair was wild and shaggy on her shoulders.

Thorvard yawned and said, "What do you wish me to do? Why must you always be making me do things when I want only a quiet life?"

She rushed at him and struck him. Then she screamed out, "You are not fit to be my husband. You are a coward and I shall divorce you before all the folk. I own everything and when you are no longer my husband, you will become a slave in this settlement. I will see to it that you suffer, lay-a-bed; oh yes, you shall suffer. Even the thralls will mock you."

Thorvard no longer wanted to sleep. He rose and said, "Very well, I cannot stand against you. Though I wish to God I had never married you. What am I to do?"

She smiled thinly and said, "Bring your most trusted men and follow me. There is no need for you to think. Just do as I say."

And when they got to the brothers' huts, she said, "Now inside with you and catch them while they lie in bed. Lay the ax on them hard. I will see that no harm comes to any of you."

The men had no stomach for the job they had to do, but they did it. There were five women in the other huts round about, and they heard the commotion and looked through their windows and saw what had happened in the dawn light. Freydis said to her husband, "Now you can make a clean sweep of the witnesses, then we will go back and eat our breakfast. The cold has made me quite hungry."

But at this even Thorvard shrank back. He flung his ax onto the ground. "I will go so far but no farther," he said. "I have never hurt a woman in my life."

Freydis picked up the ax and said, "The more fool you, then; they might have had more respect for you if you had. Now watch all the doors, I do not want any of them to get away before I have been to visit them."

And when she came back at last, her gown was sodden with something more than snow. She flung Thorvard's ax to him and said, "That is not a bad blade, but I prefer a thinner shaft that I can get my fingers round. I have quite small hands, you know, husband."

He looked at them and shuddered. Then Freydis led the men back to her huts. They were terrified at what they had done, but she stopped once and said to them, "You will be well paid, my friends. But do not breathe a word of this to anyone, or I shall come visiting you too, when you do not expect it. I am not the daughter of Eirik Redhand for nothing."

In her kitchen she burned the blood-stained gown, put on a white woolen one, and got back into bed. To Thorvard she said, "Stop shaking, you fool. There are no witnesses. No one knows who did it."

Thorvard leaned against the wall shaking. "I know," he said, "and that is enough for me. I shall never be able to forget it. I shall always know. Do not touch me with those hands."

And when the crime was discovered, Karlsefni knew too, but he could not bring Freydis to justice because, by the law of Greenland, there had to be witnesses to come forward and say that they saw a thing happen, and Freydis had made sure that there were none. Or, at least, none who dared speak of what they had seen, and had helped to do.

After this a shadow fell over the settlement by the lakeside and now all folk barred their doors at night and slept with an ax or sword beside the bed.

THE SKIN BOATS 20

But when spring came, and the sun shone, and the snows vanished as though they had never fallen, the shadow lifted a little and the folk began to smile again. Gudrid had a little boy and they named him Snorri. He was the first child to be born in Vinland and was such a fine boy that all the settlers crowded round him and wished him a happy and long life.

Freydis wanted to hold him, but Gudrid held him close to her and would not let that woman lay a finger on him. Freydis smiled down at her starkly and whispered, "Please yourself, my dear. Perhaps when my own baby is born it will be a boy. And perhaps, in time to come, my son will lay more than a finger on this little Snorri of yours. I say no more."

This troubled Gudrid and made her weep, but, as the weather improved, something happened that drove all thoughts of Freydis out of her mind. Early one morning, when the settlers were outside the stockade tethering their beasts for grazing, they heard a strange sound like corn being threshed with flails. It came closer and closer, and then, round a headland in the lake, nine skin boats rode slowly, very low in the water, and full of small men. Their faces were broad and dark skinned, their hair was coarse and black, their cheekbones were so high that their eyes looked evil. Those who were not paddling these boats shook rattlesticks with a round movement of the hands.

The settlers ran to tell Karlsefni, who said, "Do nothing to offend them. I do not know who they may be, but they sound to be much like those who shot the arrow into Thorvald."

Freydis shouted out, "Then show yourself to be a man. Kill them in revenge. They are only Skraelings. Go on, take their heads."

Karlsefni said quietly, "My name is not Thorvard."

Then he got his white shield, which signified peace, and went out of the stockade down to the waterside and waved to the men in the boats. They did not wave back, so he called out to them and smiled. But they just sat there, gazing at him, like images. Then one of them made a sharp barking sound and the rattles started again. The boats turned in one movement and then made their way slowly up the lake and round the headland.

When these strange men had gone the settlers came out and stared after them. Karlsefni said, "Well, now we know that we are not the only folk who sail on this lake. I thought that this place was too good to be true. What are we to do?"

Some of the folk said that they should tar the longships and set out for Greenland again while they could, but a few of the young men said that they were in favor of waiting a while to see what happened. Freydis spoke again and said, "If you turn tail and run before a few black-faced savages, then you can go home alone, Karlsefni. Here I am, and here I stay. If you cannot rule this settlement, then I can. Make up your mind."

Karlsefni turned away from her and said to the people, "We will stay for a while, and if they come again and are too many for us, then we will go aboard and make for Greenland. In the meantime we will chop down other trees and make a stockade that will keep out more than wolves."

Now everyone worked with a will, as though they had not much time to spare, or words either. A heavy silence hung over the settlement and few seemed anxious to break it.

Thorhall and Bjarni did not help to build the stockade. They went into the forge and put a good edge on their axes. That was their work.

Bjarni said to Thorhall, "How will it turn out, friend?"

Thorhall said, "The way it always does. The one who gets his knock in first wins. There is no more to life than that. There is no mystery about it. Life is really a very simple affair, if men would only let it be so."

Then he began to sing as he honed his ax blade. The words of his song were very ancient, not even Bjarni knew them.

SECOND TIME

Most of the settlers made their own plans. Some dug deep pits in their houses where the women and children could shelter if the place were fired. But many women said they would rather fight beside the men and practiced with ax and spear. They were not allowed swords, because no woman was thought skillful enough to manage that pretty weapon.

The youngest Vikings laid in a good store of arrows and went about swaggering with their belts stuffed full of knives and swords, as though they looked forward to a second visit from the Skraelings.

Karlsefni went to Freydis and said to her, "Now, Eirik's-daughter, let us get one thing clear in our heads. If these Skraelings come again, I do not want to see you anywhere, giving advice to the young firebrands in this village."

Freydis said stubbornly, "Someone must advise them, otherwise they will waste their arrows."

Karlsefni said coldly, "I am the master here and I shall tell all the folk what to do. If you step but one pace out of position, I swear I will make you, and your husband, pay for what happened to the two brothers and the women. You shall hang from the highest tree in the forest."

Freydis drew in her nostrils and said, her eyes glinting like ice, "I don't mind hanging—if you can hang me, merchant. But do you mind hanging—if I can hang you?"

Karlsefni went from her house, hearing her mad laughter following him. He told Gudrid what had been said. She bowed her head and answered, "My husband, let us sail away home. Let us take our little son and be thankful. This is an awful place. When folk come here they turn to brutish beasts. I want to go back to Norway, where I was born. I shall die of grief if we do not go back. I cannot bring up a family in these wild places, no matter where. I dream every night of the terrors in Greenland and Iceland, but here worst of all. Let us go back, Karlsefni."

He looked at her patiently and said, "Dearest love, what can I do, with all the folk depending on me? I cannot leave them, not even for you and for my little son. If I did, when I sat in my warm hall in Bergen, I should think of these poor souls stranded among savages for the rest of my days. No morsel of food or drink would pass down my throat, for I should be a murderer. I could not call myself a Christian after that."

Gudrid got up from her stool and paced about a while. Then she went to him and said, "Husband, forgive me, I am not a very good wife for a Viking to have. I am too afraid of what might happen to our little one. You know my story as well as anyone: how I stood in the sea on that reef, with all the dying men beside me, shouting to be taken off to dry land. There I lost my husband Thorir, while we were both young ones. Then poor Thorstein Eiriksson tended me when I had the plague, and died for me, for his dream of me. So many folk died there, in Greenland, because of me. When I married you, I hoped we might go back to Norway and live in cities among merry folk, but we came here instead, and here we had our first child. Karlsefni, I have seen too much of death. I wish to see no more. Please take me home."

Then Karlsefni rose and put his arms round her. And he said, "My love, I have been selfish, the way men are. I thought only of glory on the sea and profit on the land. Yes, we will go home to Norway. We will go to where there are streets and churches and folk dressed in clean linen. My dream is over.

Forgive me for imposing it on you. I can see clearly at last and I thank you, Gudrid."

He bent and kissed her cheek, then strode out.

Thorhall met him at the door and said briefly, "They have come back. The lake is black with them. You must be deaf if you cannot hear their rattle-sticks. I can hardly hear myself speaking to you."

Karlsefni said, "Why do you carry an ax in your hand?"

Thorhall said, "You thwarted me once, over the whale meat, master. This time old Thor shall have his dues, or you will go headless to the Heaven you talk about. Come on, my lord, we will go to meet these savages, and I shall be close behind you. Never forget that. I do not mind dying—but now I strongly suspect that you do. Move, my lord, move!"

When Karlsefni saw the massed canoes, his heart sank. It seemed that a man could walk dry shod across the lake on them. He turned to Thorhall and said, "We cannot fight this swarm. There would be twenty to one, even if we gave our women weapons to wield."

Thorhall smiled and said, "Let us leave one good story for the world to hear then. Let the two of us— a Thorman and a Christman—rip off our shirts and make the old baresark run at them. We could rattle the heads of a few monkeys before they got at us, Karlsefni."

Karlsefni put out his hand and took a friendly grasp of Thorhall's beard. He shook at it, grinning for a while, then said, "You are all the better for knowing, heathen. Now, will you go back and keep a watch on Freydis? See that she does not break loose and make death for us all? I will go down to the boats and meet these folk."

Thorhall said, "You keep Freydis in order, and I will calm these savages. Why give me the hard work to do?"

But when he had had his joke he went, and Karlsefni took the white shield and strode toward the waiting canoes. The settlers watched him from the top of the stockade. For a long while he seemed to be pacing down to that crowded black lake, and no one spoke a word. Then he reached the water's edge, still smiling and pointing to his shield.

The silence was so heavy and so long that one of the Greenland women started to scream. Immediately, all the eyes of the dark folk in the canoes lifted to see where the noise came from. The woman's husband clapped his hand over her mouth and carried her away into her house.

Then slowly the first of the canoes half-turned and rode into shore. The man who came out of it first was short and squat and very thickly built. On his legs and feet he wore white deerskin boots that reached up to the thigh. His body was clothed in a glistening black bearskin. Its hood lay about his neck. His coarse black hair shone with fat. His copper-colored skin was daubed with bars of blue and white clay. He walked toward Karlsefni for a time, then stopped a pace away from him and gazed into his eyes. The Norwegian stood his ground and kept nodding and smiling down at the Skraeling. Then suddenly the savage reached forward swiftly, took the white shield and flung it behind him, over the lake. It was caught by warriors in the further canoes and examined. Karlsefni stood quite still while the man touched his face and hair, then suddenly took hold of his red cloth tunic and began to pull at it.

At this, Karlsefni slowly withdrew and, slipping off the tunic, offered it to the Skraeling. The man took it, glared at him for an instant, then signed with his hand to the others in his canoe. They came forward with a great pile of sables and laid them at Karlsefni's feet. For his tunic they had given him enough fur to buy a longship. He felt sure that they were joking with him, meaning to kill him in a moment.

But now they were laughing by their leader's canoe, and sawing at the red tunic with their stone knives. Karlsefni watched it fall into six strips, then to be wound about the heads of the Skraelings.

Thorhall at the stockade saw this too and said,

"Why, the poor fools only want red stuff to wrap round their silly heads. Get out all the red cloth we have. It is a new color to them, so they want it."

The settlers did this, and laid out the cloth by the stockade, standing beside it to collect their sables and other furs.

Then the canoes came in, line by line to the bank, and the Skraelings stepped from one to the other and so to land. They passed by Karlsefni in droves, but did not touch him or his heap of furs. They were too busy with the heavy bundles they carried on their backs.

THE BLACK BULL 22

By the time Karlsefni had got back to the stockade a brisk trade was going on. At first the settlers were giving at least decent value for the furs they took, but soon the red cloth began to run short, and now many of the Greenlanders were cutting their cloth into small strips and trading it for the same amount of furs. Yet the Skraelings still took what they were offered and did not question the small amount they got.

In the rush to barter the cloth, the settlers had left the stockade gates open and now Karlsefni, seeing danger, called out, "Do not let them in, lads. Stand in a body before the entrance. Do not let them in. We should never get them out again."

But already the chief and his four friends were inside and looking at the piled weapons of the settlers. One of the youths bent and took up a sword, turning it over with great curiosity. And at that point great Thorhall in his black bearskin stepped forth and took the sword gently from the youth's hand, offering him instead a clay bowl of cow's milk.

The Skraeling took it and tasted it, then gave it to the chief. After he had drunk the bowl dry, he turned to Thorhall and held it out again. Thorhall said, "Nay, master, I'm no kitchen thrall to go running for a monkey's pleasure."

But Karlsefni called out, "Give them some more, you fool. Lead them away from the weapon heap."

And Thorhall did this. Soon the settlers were trading a bowl of milk for a bundle of sables. And still the Skraelings seemed quite happy about the trading.

Bjarni said to Thorhall, "There must be a catch in it somewhere. We have robbed them right and left, and still they are grinning and chattering like apes. I have just bartered three cups of milk for the value of a year's farming in Breidafjord. This does not make sense. A hard bargain is a hard bargain—but when it gets to this pitch, I begin to wonder who is mad, the Skraelings or myself."

Thorhall still smiled, but whispered between tight

jaws, "Be ready for anything. Keep your sword where you can reach it in a hurry. Give them some more milk; if that is what they want, why should we break our hearts? They are the losers, not us."

Now while all this jostling and shouting was going on, Gudrid sat behind her house nursing little Snorri and wishing it could all be over so that they could take ship for Norway once again. For a time there was a deal of shouting and scuffling nearby and Gudrid started to run inside the house in alarm. But the quarrel soon died down and Bjarni came up to her, roaring with laughter and throwing a bundle of otter pelts toward her. "These are for the little chieftain," he said. "They will buy him a pony back home. I got them for a broken old cloak pin that wasn't worth a sniff. Oh, I shall like living here after all. Inside three years I shall be rich enough to go back to Iceland and buy all the farms for myself. How do you like the sound of 'King Bjarni'?"

Gudrid laughed and said, "Well, it would be different. There has never been one before that I have heard of."

Now, in the middle of all this jesting, a most unlucky thing happened. Some of the Skraelings had made their way past the settlement to the woods behind it, where the Greenlanders had put their sheep and cattle for safety. Suddenly Karlsefni's black bull, a touchy beast at the best of times, sniffed the musky scent of the Skraelings and broke his thong halter in fright. He was known to be a stupid brute who attacked anything that made him afraid. And now he came through the undergrowth with one Skraeling hanging from his horns and another being trampled underfoot.

Their chieftain saw this and shouted to one of his henchmen. This man raised his short bow and let loose an arrow. But, in his haste, the aim was wrong and the shaft only glanced off the bull's forehead. Then there was trouble to be sure. The beast ran in upon the chieftain and his party, toppling them left and right, then goring at them as they rolled on the ground, and at last kneeling on the leader until he was dead.

Karlsefni rushed up and beat the bull off with a stick, but the damage was done. As though a cloth had been swept from a feast board, the Skraelings had run down to their canoes again. They sat in them like ghosts for a while, in deathly silence, then all at once their rattles started up once more, they swung round, and with swift strokes of the paddles, they went back up the lake and round the headland.

Thorhall came up to Karlsefni and said heavily, "Well, friend, there will be trouble to be sure."

Karlsefni nodded. "Aye," he said, "the next time they come it will not be with furs to trade. It was a mistake to bring that bull of mine. Yet I thought I was doing right at the time."

Thorhall said, "It's the same with us all, whomever we pray to, friend. Let us go back inside the stockade and make ready for war. We have been forced into it by a twist of fate."

THIRD TIME

No one slept that night. Instead, they piled wood against the inside of the stockade and covered their houses with damp turf so that they could not be fired with tar arrows. The women brought in all the water they could, in buckets from the lake, and the men rounded up the cattle and penned them behind the huts. Only Karlsefni's bull was left outside, for it was thought that he of all creatures would be best able to keep the Skraelings at bay if they came in the darkness.

But they waited until dawn; and when they did come, not even Karlsefni's bull could have kept them back for long, for they poured down the lake like a black torrent, shaking their rattlesticks a different way this time so as to give the impression of myriads of crickets all shrieking out at once. It was a noise that set the teeth on edge and made even the bravest man want to run away as fast as his legs could carry him.

Gudrid heard it and said, "Will you lend me your dagger, husband?"

Karlsefni asked, "What, do you wish to go out with the men and face these savages?"

She shook her head and said, her eyes closed, "No, husband. But if they break in now I have a good idea what will happen to us all. I shall see to Snorri and myself. Will you promise to look after your side of the business? I could not bear to think of them mishandling you."

Karlsefni gave her the dagger and said, "I promise, though I hope it may not come to that. Like you, I have a strong wish to set eyes on Bergen again."

She smiled up at him sadly, then shook her head. "That is just a dream, husband," she said. "We shall never see Norway now. I was talking like a foolish young girl when I thought we might. We are at the edge of the world, and this is our end."

Then Karlsefni went to get the Vikings into position. He had decided that it would be best not to keep all the men inside the stockade but to send out a party of the seasoned fighters to delay the Skraelings a while and to knock some of the heart out of them. The spot he chose to defend was a narrow stretch of land with an inlet of the lake on one side and a dense grove of trees on the other. This time the men took their red shields, to signify war, and ran forward baying like hounds to strike fear into the hearts of the Skraelings.

Thorhall ran beside Karlsefni and Bjarni at the front. He said as they ran, "The sooner we get this over, the sooner we can sit down and enjoy a good dinner."

Bjarni said, "I have been craving for a dish of pig meat and onions all the morning. When I get back to Iceland, one of these days, I will start a trade in onions if I can get them to grow. There is no finer fruit than the onion."

Thorhall said, "Onions are not a fruit. You must be mad."

They stopped then to argue about this, but one of the other men, a fierce fighter called Thorbrand, called out, "Get on with you both, Karlsefni's bull cannot hold them back forever."

He was right. The first rank of Skraelings paused a while before the bellowing black beast, but then, pushed from behind, they overwhelmed him and, though he did great work that day, soon there was little left of him but horns and tattered hide.

Then, as the Vikings took up their places, the Skraelings halted and stared at them as though wondering how best to attack them. Thorhall yelled, "Come on, little monkeys, we cannot wait forever."

At the front of the Skraeling army stood a tall and handsome young chieftain, his long black hair set off with ribbons and his arms with bands of red copper. Thorhall pulled a light ax from his belt and said, "Redbeard, guide my aim!" Then he threw the ax at the chieftain, but it fell just a few inches short and stuck into the ground between the Skraeling's feet.

The youth stared at it for an instant, then bent and picked it up, looking at it curiously. Other young men gathered round and felt its edge and its shaft, nodding and laughing. One of them, much like the chieftain in features, tried to take it from him; but, with a smile, the young warrior pretended to strike at his companion with the ax. Its balance was so different from what he had been used to, the blade plunged forward and struck the other Skraeling who fell dead straightway. At this, a great hissing went up from the host, and all the laughter stopped. The young chieftain gave a loud cry, then turned and flung the ax far away into the lake.

The Vikings saw the splash it made, and Bjarni said, "Well, you've lost your ax now, brother."

Karlsefni said, "Close your ranks and lock your shields, or we shall lose more than an ax very soon."

The Skraelings came on like a winter's wave, but at first the Greenlanders were able to push them back with their red shields until they could cut them down. It fell to Thorhall to kill the young chieftain. He said, "That is in payment for my best ax that you threw away."

Sharp work was done both with sword and ax, and the spear did not go without its victims. Soon the narrow space between lake and wood was heaped high with Skraelings, yet they came on.

Bjarni said, "I still say that the onion is a fruit." He was fighting three Skraelings at the time. No one answered him—there were other things to do. Thorbrand gave a good account of himself and held at least six savages at bay, until one of them took careful aim from close range and flung a small flint ax at him. It stuck firmly into Thorbrand's head and he said to Karlsefni, "I think I will take a rest, master. Put someone else in my place." Then he fell dead.

When the Vikings saw this, they gave ground. And now the Skraelings began to use a fearful weapon on them. It was a form of catapult, made by wrapping a round stone in a sheep's stomach and by slinging it at the end of a long pole. These missiles set up a deep whirring in the air, and when they landed did great damage. Now so many of them flew through the air that the Vikings backed away from them. Karlsefni shouted out, "Stand firm, lads, or they will force us into the lake."

Thorhall, who was hobbling from a rock that had bounded against his leg, said, "That's all very well, master, but these little stones they keep throwing are an annoyance. Why can't they come up and fight like men?"

The Vikings tried to stand then, but another hail of missiles flung them back, and now it seemed that with one more push the Skraelings would have them in the water, unable to defend themselves.

Bjarni said sorrowfully, "I must say farewell to my dish of onions. And I *was* looking forward to them."

But just at that moment a strange thing happened. Running from the dense grove of trees, her hair streaming and her heavy skirts hitched up, came Freydis. She was screaming wordlessly and ripping at her gown like a madwoman. At first the Skraelings gazed at her bewildered, and she raced past them to where Thorbrand lay dead with the flint ax in his head and snatched up the sword he had dropped. Five young braves ran at her then, laughing and leveling their spears. But Freydis let out a high-pitched shriek and went to meet the tallest of them. With her first slash she took off the head of his spear. With her second, she left him headless. Then, swinging, she did the same to the next man. And each time she squealed and slapped the reeking blade on her bare arm, as though counting her victims.

Only one other man came at her. He was older than the rest and his hair had gray streaks in it.

His ax was already poised for the cast when she put Thorbrand's blade right through his body, then, raising her bare foot, she kicked him off the point. He fell back four paces before falling into the coarse grasses.

At this the other Skraelings turned and fled. Some of them even dropped their weapons. For a while, Freydis ran after them, but Karlsefni raced to stop her and put his arms about her. She struggled with him for a space, then leaned against him weeping, the heavy sword forgotten now.

Thorhall said stark-faced to Bjarni, "Well, I never liked the lass much till now, but from this day I will bow my head before her when she passes by. Old Eirik Redhand could not have done better than his daughter did."

Karlsefni came back with Freydis. He led her before the men and said, "This is a woman. She has done many evil things, but today she has wiped away the stains on her name. Take her back to the stockade, Thorhall, and see that she is cared for. We will push on against the Skraelings."

But Thorhall said, "Turn round, Karlsefni, and see what we can see. There are no Skraelings to fight. They have run down to their boats and are pushing off."

In the settlement, Gudrid now tended to Freydis, who should have been resting because of the baby she was to have. Karlsefni was outside now, talking to all the assembled folk.

He said, "Well, a bull started this fight and a woman finished it. It seems that the best we men can do is to set the ships on course back for Greenland. My mind is now made up. This is the end of our settlement here in Vinland. No man could ever live in safety and freedom again among these Skraelings. We will go home."

And all the folk took up his words and cried out, "Yes, master, we will go home."

THE LONG WAY BACK 24

It was a long way back, and not the best time of the year. The voyagers took what timber they could, and loaded the furs on top of it. They did not bother with vines, for now the very name of them was awful to the ear. In many ways it was a sad trip, and most of the sheep and cattle had to be slaughtered for food as the boats tacked northward before a treacherous wind.

At one place they put in for fresh water and, seeing a family of Skraelings resting, fell on them and butchered them without mercy, for now they looked on these folk as nothing but wild beasts.

Then winter drove the voyagers ashore, onto a headland where deer grazed and the hunting was easy. But even here, misfortune struck, for Thorhall, boasting that he could find a good wind by snapping his fingers, turned his prow out of the haven and was swept off into the empty sea, toward the east, before even he could get the helm hard round.

The others saw him go, always scudding away smaller and smaller, and they even heard his loud voice crying out to Thor for help, long after the fogs had curled round his ship and had hidden it from view.

Bjarni watched his old mate go and said, "Farewell, voyager. May the Irish kings come down to greet thee bearing gold."

No one spoke of Thorhall after that. He had been a gruff man but a loyal one, and his loss was a great weight on them all.

Some days later Karlsefni went up along the coast seeking fresh water. He put ashore in a small boat, and the men were just filling their waterskins when a very small Skraeling jumped up from the reeds by the creek and shot a very small arrow at them. It struck a man called Oddi in the groin. For a moment he looked at this little wound, then laughed and said, "You chase that Skraeling and don't fear for me. I have enough fat on me to withstand such a little arrow." Then he pulled the shaft out, and fell forward dead. His comrades went after the Skraeling, but found no trace of him.

After that the ice came and the men had to get back as fast as they could to winter quarters. And it was no pleasant winter, because, by now, many of the younger women began to start quarrels among the men, telling spiteful tales and carrying gossip.

Bjarni came to Karlsefni and said, "Shipmaster, far be it for me to tell you your trade, but it is my opinion that the sooner we can set sail again, the better. I know that the winds are best in spring, but if we wait as long as that, many who are now alive will be dead, from one thing or another. I say that we should set course as soon as the year turns."

Karlsefni nodded. "We will do that," he said. "It is very risky, but it would be even more risky to stay here."

So they waited for the first good wind that would swing them round toward Greenland. And when it came, they set off again. They put in at Slabland for water and there found a party of very strange Skraelings, much smaller than all the others and very dark in the skin. These folk ran away swiftly when the Vikings approached but left behind them two children, very thin and miserable looking. Karlsefni had them baptized and handed them over to the young women to look after, so that they should have something to keep their minds away from gossip and malice.

When they put off the next time, toward Green-

land, all went well until they were out of sight of
land, and then the wind dropped completely and
left them wallowing around in a dead sea.

By now the men were too weary to row, and the
sails hung limply without a breath of breeze in
them. Day after day the boats sat. Sometimes they
came close enough together for the men to talk to
one another. Sometimes they drifted slowly apart,
out of earshot, almost out of sight.

It was at this time that Bjarni ran into trouble.
His ship was an old one and near the end of its life.
Most of the timbers below the waterline were worm
riddled, but the ship could have got back to Greenland if they had not been so delayed.

At noon one day Bjarni's longship began to sink
slowly in the green water. Men could not bale fast
enough to keep the level down. So, while there was
still time, the folk aboard drew lots to see who
should go in the small tow boat, since there was not
room enough for them all.

Bjarni had the good luck to gain for himself a
place in the boat, and he took it without question,
for the lots had been drawn fairly. But just as he
was about to give the order to draw away from the
longship, to avoid being drawn down by the whirl-
pool it would make on sinking, a young Icelander
still aboard came to the shield rail and shouted
down, "Hey, Bjarni, when you persuaded me to

leave my father's farm and come with you to Vinland, you swore that I would be taken care of. Is this how you keep your word?"

Bjarni answered, "We drew lots fairly. I can see no other way. What do you suggest?"

The youth cried out, "I suggest we change places."

Bjarni said, "Well, if you are so determined to live, I will not stand in your way, lad. Throw down the rope and I'll take your place."

The young man jumped into the tow boat and it pulled away from the doomed ship. Then a water current seemed to catch it and sweep it toward the empty south, as though a hand were guiding it from beneath the green water.

Bjarni in the stricken longship watched it go, then said to those about him, "Well, friends, at least they won't have to bother about rowing. They will be in Ireland before they know it, and I hope that old Thorhall is there to greet them."

The longship began to groan and shudder beneath his feet, almost throwing him off balance, but he still held onto the mast and said, "There is no need for long faces, brothers. We have not had a bad life. At least we have seen more than those lay-a-beds in Greenland and Iceland. And, when you think of it, which of us would ever be content again in a quiet farmstead? Nay, we should always be dreaming of Vinland. Then, one day, we should try to reach our dream once more—and so the winter, or the Skraelings, or the sea would have us in the end. Better to go now, with no more argument. Keep your heavy boots and jackets on, so as to make a quick job of it. We could not hope to swim as far as the other ships, even if we could swim; and I, for one, cannot. To tell the truth, I have always been afraid of deep water!"

While they were laughing at this, the longship suddenly cried out as though its timbers had a human voice. Then, weighted with water, it flung its carved prow high into the air and slid down tail first, setting up a great swirl. The folk went with it in silence, and not one came up to the top again.

From a distance, Karlsefni watched this helplessly, then said, "Christ have mercy on them, and may He let us die as bravely when our time comes."

He had hardly spoken when a great wind got up from the west and shrieked in his sail tops. It was as though the loss of Bjarni's longship were a payment for that wind.

So all the scattered ships swung round before the wind and headed for Greenland, and it was not many days before they sailed up Eiriksfjord again.

THE LAST WINTER 25

The months had gone by. Leif Eiriksson sat with Thorgils by the fire, only the two of them in the hall at Brattahlid. Leif said, "They did not stay with us long, Tyrkir and Gudrid and Karlsefni. I should have grown fond of that little boy, Snorri. He has the makings of a seafarer in him."

Thorgils said, "His father will see that the boy becomes a good solid merchant in Bergen. There will be no seafaring for Snorri. And who would risk the empty seas with the sort of cargo they have taken back with them—furs, timber, ivory? They need not lift a finger to work again for the rest of their lives. Vinland has made them rich."

Leif nodded sadly. "It has made me very poor," he said. "It has taken all my family from me, one way or another. Yet it has given you to me. I must be thankful."

Thorgils said, "No man gets through this life without suffering. We must learn to make the best of it."

Leif thought a while, then said, "Sometimes I regret banishing Freydis and her husband and baby to the other side of Greenland. Did I do right, my son?"

Thorgils smiled and answered, "Who am I to say? She was certainly a brave woman, but there were such evil rumors about her. . . . Yes, I think you did right. But let us not sit indoors over the fire like old men. Let us go out into the sunshine while there is still a little of it left before the snow comes."

They went off together onto the hillside above the fjord, and there Leif saw a place where the careless thralls had knocked down a part of the stone wall around the farm boundary and had not set it up again.

He said, "There, you see, a farmer always has work to do. He can never trust his servants to look after things properly. Come, give a hand and we will put this wall up again."

Thorgils tried to stop him, but the old man was already bending and heaving at a great round boulder that had rolled out of position. "Here, let me do that, father," said Thorgils, stepping forward.

But he was too late. Suddenly, as Leif strained at the weight, it seemed that his ears were filled with the rushing of a high wind, and in the midst of this there was a sound like a ship's rope snapping in his head. He fell face downward onto the hard ground and could not get up again.

When he woke, he was lying in the wall bed at Brattahlid and Thorgils was bending over him, holding a cup of warm spiced wine near his lips. Leif saw that the fire had been built up and that the dark sky pressed close against the window holes.

He said, "I dreamed there was a woman standing over me, but whether it was your mother or mine I cannot tell. Was there a woman here?"

Thorgils shook his head. "I saw no woman," he said. "Only the shadows thrown by the firelight."

Leif tried to sip the wine, but it ran down his chin. He said, "My mother always said that a strange terror would come down on us from the north. You know many things, my son. Do you know what that terror is?"

Thorgils said slowly, "It will become very cold. The icecap will move down toward us and smother the land. It will freeze the seas. The seals will come south in fear of it. They will come in great hordes to escape the white winter of the north."

Leif began to laugh then and said, "Why, that is no terror. It will mean that we only have to walk into the stackyard to get meat for our dinner. That is no terror, son."

Thorgils rose and went to the hall door and, opening it a little way, gazed out in the moonlight over the snow-covered hillside. All at once the sheep in the byre began to bleat as though they were afraid of something, and as Thorgils stared he saw a number of dark shapes moving about, bent double, in the shadow of the stockade. They ran in silence and were like no men he had ever seen before. Quietly he closed the thick door and drew the bars across it at top and bottom. Then he went back to his chair near the fire and sat looking at Leif.

The old man turned his eyes on him wearily and said, "Why are the sheep crying out? They are locked up warmly against the winter and have food enough."

Thorgils answered, "You know what sheep are—even a shadow will frighten them."

Leif smiled and said, "Aye, that is true. They are silly beasts, though we could not do without them."

He fingered his sheepskin coverlet for a while, then said quite clearly, "Why do you sit with that great iron dirk across your knees? Lay it aside and sit in comfort, my son. You are in your own house, you are not in Vinland waiting for Skraelings to break in. Lay the dirk aside, Thorgils, and be at ease."

So Thorgils obeyed Leif and stood the dirk beside a coffer chest, where he could reach it quickly.

Then Leif began to tell him the old story of how he had once sat beside King Olaf in the hall in Norway. He tried to remember the names of courtiers who had been there, but his memory failed him and he clucked with annoyance.

At last he looked across at Thorgils and said sharply, "You are not listening, my boy. No, you are not listening."

Thorgils smiled at him starkly. "Yes, I am listening," he said. "I am listening very carefully indeed."

But he did not tell the old man what he was listening for. He could not bring himself to tell Leif what was now lurking in the darkness at the other side of the barred door.

AFTERWORD

In a way, this is quite a sad story, though it ended happily for Karlsefni and his family. He made a great profit from his cargo, and even sold the prow of his longship, which Tyrkir had carved from Vinland maple. Gudrid became very popular with the Norwegian nobility, who all wanted to know what life was like at the other side of the world.

After a time Karlsefni and Gudrid had another son, named Thorbjorn, and settled down on a prosperous farm in Iceland. When Karlsefni died at last, Snorri (the first white American), became a rich man and had a church built. Gudrid made a pilgrimage to Rome and later devoted herself to a religious life.

As for the settlements in Greenland that Eirik had founded, they gradually decayed. A new ice age set in and life became very wretched there. The Greenlanders could not get away to other places, nor, because of icebergs, could ships from Iceland and Norway reach them. Perhaps worst of all, the Eskimos came down, following the migrating seals. Theirs were the dark shapes that Thorgils had seen in the shadow of the stockade. They either killed or enslaved the settlers, and those who survived suffered starvation and disease.

In 1492, the same year in which Columbus made his discovery of America, a papal letter was written that contained these words: "Greenland is said to be an island near the edge of the world. Its people have no bread, wine, or oils. They live on dried fish and milk. Because of the ice that surrounds this island, no ship has sailed there for the last eighty years. No bishop or priest has visited that place for the same period of time."

HENRY TREECE